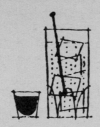

THE CALVERT PARTY ENCYCLOPEDIA

YOUR COMPLETE GUIDE TO HOME ENTERTAINING

COMPILED AND EDITED BY
CALVERT DISTILLERS COMPANY

CALVERT EXTRA • 86 PROOF • BLENDED WHISKEY • 65% GRAIN NEUTRAL SPIRITS
CANADIAN LORD CALVERT • IMPORTED CANADIAN WHISKY • A BLEND
80 PROOF • CALVERT GIN • 90 PROOF • DISTILLED FROM 100% AMERICAN GRAIN
CALVERT COCKTAILS • MARTINI • 70 PROOF • WHISKEY SOUR,
MANHATTAN, DAIQUIRI • 60 PROOF • CALVERT DISTILLING CO.

THE CALVERT PARTY ENCYCLOPEDIA

YOUR COMPLETE
GUIDE TO
HOME ENTERTAINING

TABLE OF CONTENTS

INTRODUCTION

HERE'S TO A HAPPY PARTY!

Parties help you relax and spend enjoyable hours in good company. When you bring your friends together for an evening at your home, your aim is to blend a group which will enjoy each other's company and make for a pleasurable evening.

People are one of the elements in making a party successful. Another is the way you blend the little touches that make you an outstanding host or hostess. Your food, and, of course, your refreshments, all help add up to the kind of party your guests talk about and remember.

This book is intended for your pleasure, so please allow us to point out the moral of our story way up front. You are a blender in everything you do. You blend your friends, your food, your decorations; the very clothes you wear are probably blended of the new miracle fabrics.

The art of blending in its highest form is achieved when Calvert produces its famous Calvert Extra, the Soft Whiskey. With a masterly touch Calvert blends a selection of choice whiskies and spirits. Some are chosen for vigor... others for bouquet... still others for delicacy of flavor.

This book, too, is a blend of essential ingredients to help you plan a successful party. Here is your complete guidebook to modern entertaining. In it you'll find a world of new, novel and exciting party ideas.

In fact — for a change of pace once in a while — you might consider holding your party out, using the facilities of your favorite tavern, hotel, club or restaurant.

Look into the following pages. You'll find fascinating and helpful ideas and information — the latest cocktails — the easiest recipes — and the tastiest canapes. Be sure to include Calvert Extra, the Soft Whiskey. It's the first hard liquor that's not "hard."

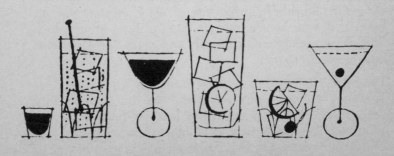

CHAPTER ONE

UNHURRIED PARTY PLANNING...
THE CLUE TO SUCCESS!

HANDY HINTS FOR THE HOST OR HOSTESS

"Plan Ahead" is a good motto for party giving. It often means the difference between a great party — and an ordinary one.

Here's a handy guide to help you plan the perfect party. How much liquor will you need? What about glasses, food and other items? Follow the suggestions in this chapter. You'll be ready for everything. Most important: you'll assure a good time for all — including yourself.

Party Planning

Decide how many guests you plan to invite. This is the most important factor in party planning. It will help you plan in advance how much of everything you need. Cocktail parties are the easiest type to give. They are casual and friendly. Guests provide their own entertainment.

Mixing Drinks

Follow the exact measurements in a recipe. Two dashes of bitters might drown out the flavor of a cocktail that one dash was designed to cultivate.

Serving Drinks

Decide ahead of time the routine for making and serving drinks and cocktails. It is traditionally the host's function . . . or the host can appoint a friend. A hostess can ask a male guest. Have a fixed place to make drinks and serve them.

Serve drinks as far away from food as possible. This avoids traffic jams. At smaller parties, after serving guests their first drinks, suggest that they make their own refills.

Deciding Which Drinks To Serve

Drinks should fit the occasion. Highballs are always appropriate. At dinner parties, you might serve cocktails before dinner, highballs after dinner.

At Christmas, New Year's and other Holiday parties, Egg Nog, Tom 'N' Jerry, Milk Punch are traditional. In summer, the long drinks, particularly the Collins family and Coolers are welcome.

Consider the size of the party when deciding upon drinks to be served. Punch is often an easy solution to providing a continuous supply of drinks to many guests at one time.

Greeting Guests

Greet guests warmly at the door. Show them where to hang their wraps, or take the wraps from them yourself.

At larger parties, if guests are strangers, introduce them to at least a few of your other guests. At smaller parties, introduce all arrivals to everyone, unless you are sure they know each other. It is no mistake to introduce people who already know one another.

Equipment For The Bar

Here is a checklist of items you'll want for a complete bar.

1 Cocktail Shaker with Top
1 Bottle Opener
1 Corkscrew
1 Set of Ice Tongs
1 Bar Strainer
1 Large Mixing Pitcher
1 Jigger (1½ ounces)
1 Muddler
1 Lemon/Lime Squeezer
1 Stainless Steel Knife
1 Ice Bucket
1 Serving Tray
1 Long-Handled Mixing Spoon
Coasters
Stirrers
Napkins

Glassware

Here is a list of standard glassware. The number of each particular size of glass you will need will depend upon the number of guests.

Cocktail Glass	3 or 4 ounces
Jigger	1½ ounces
Old Fashioned Glass	4 to 6 ounces
Sour Glass	5 ounces
Champagne Glass	5 to 6 ounces
Collins Glass	12 ounces
Highball Glass	6 to 8 ounces
Julep Glass	10 to 12 ounces
Brandy Glass	3 ounces
Cordial Glass	2 ounces
Sherry Wine Glass	4 ounces
Standard Wine Glass	6 ounces

Correct Measures

1 Gallon (U.S.)	128 ounces
½ Gallon	64 ounces
1 Quart	32 ounces
1 Fifth (4/5 Quart)	25.6 ounces
¾ Quart	24 ounces
1 Pint	16 ounces
1 Tenth	12.8 ounces
1 Cup (½ Pint)	8 ounces
1 Jigger	1½ ounces
1 Pony	⅛ ounce
1 Dash	3 Drops

Suggested Liquor Supplies

A Basic $25 Bar

1 Fifth Calvert Extra Whiskey
1 Fifth Calvert Gin
1 Fifth Canadian Lord Calvert

1 Fifth Scotch
1 Bottle Dry Vermouth
1 Bottle Sweet Vermouth

A Basic $50 Bar

2 Fifths Calvert Extra Whiskey
2 Fifths Calvert Gin
1 Fifth Canadian Lord Calvert
1 Fifth Vodka
1 Fifth Scotch

1 Bottle Calvert Whiskey Sour
1 Bottle Calvert Daiquiri
1 Bottle Sweet Vermouth
1 Bottle Dry Vermouth

A Basic $100 Bar

4 Fifths Calvert Extra Whiskey
2 Fifths Calvert Gin
2 Fifths Scotch
2 Fifths Canadian Lord Calvert
1 Fifth Vodka
1 Fifth Light Rum
1 Fifth Brandy
1 Bottle Creme de Menthe
1 Bottle Calvert Martini
1 Bottle Calvert Manhattan
1 Bottle Calvert Whiskey Sour

1 Bottle Calvert Daiquiri
1 Bottle Calvert Margarita
1 Bottle Dry Vermouth
1 Bottle Sweet Vermouth
1 Bottle Dry Sherry
1 Bottle Triple Sec
1 Bottle Creme de Cacao
1 Bottle Aromatic Bitters
1 Bottle Grenadine
1 Bottle Maraschino Liqueur

Serving Wines

Wine is not an expensive luxury. Even though certain select chateau and vintage wines may be high in price, there are many splendid domestic and imported wines at prices within everyone's reach.

White wines are generally served cooler than red or sweet wines. When serving a chilled wine, wrap a napkin around the bottle to retard the warmth of the hand from warming the contents and to prevent dripping.

Serve wine in clear, thin glasses. Pour wine gently, never shake it.

Generally, serve white wines with fowl, game or fish. Serve red wines with red meats.

Serve dry wines prior to the dessert course. Sweet wines should be served at the close of a meal or after it.

The serving of wines may be altered according to taste or necessity.

Some of the more popular wines are:

WHITE WINES	RED WINES
Sauterne	Red Burgundy
Dry Sherry	Red Bordeaux (Claret)
Chablis	Red Chianti
Riesling	Red Rhone Valley
White Burgundy	St. Emilion
Rhine Wine	Beaujolais
Moselle	Zinfandel
Champagne	Vin Rose
Vermouth	St. Julien
White Bordeaux	Macon
Graves	Pommard
	Sparkling Burgundy

DESSERT WINES

Malaga	Chateau Yquem
Port	Madeira
Angelica	Tokay

**Hints To
Help You Be
An Expert Host**

Always use a jigger (1½ oz.) to measure your liquor. Don't guess. Your liquor will go further.

To make glassware really sparkle, wash in warm water, dry with a towel, polish with a fresh dry towel.

Chill cocktail glasses in refrigerator before serving.

Carbonated drinks should never be stirred vigorously. This releases the gas and makes the drink go flat quicker. Always hold soda bottle at an angle when opening. This preserves the sparkle and minimizes foaming over.

Thin-lipped glasses seem to make drinks taste better.

Use fresh glasses for repeats. Just a drop or two of the stale drink can ruin a fresh one.

It is difficult to dissolve sugar in liquor. Always dissolve the sugar in a few drops of water before mixing. (Sugar dissolves faster in carbonated water. You can make simple sugar syrup in advance. Mix half water, half sugar. Simmer until sugar is dissolved. Keep in refrigerator.)

When sugar is called for in a drink, use granulated sugar.

When adding an olive to a drink, always pierce it with a toothpick. Use cherries with stems. Your guests will appreciate the extra convenience.

A melted ice cube makes 2 to 2½ ounces of water. Never re-use cubes. They can spoil your next drink. To take the snowy look from ice cubes, sprinkle them with lukewarm water.

Rub the lip of your whiskey bottle with waxed paper before pouring. This prevents dripping. Except in highballs, liquor should be the last item added to a drink.

Fresh fruit juice makes a drink taste better.

To frost a cocktail glass, dip the rim of the glass in ¼ inch of lemon juice, then in granulated sugar. Pour cocktail to just below the sugar line. (Colored sugar can be made by adding vegetable dye.) If the recipe says shake . . . don't stir. If it says stir . . . don't shake.

Line up your supplies beforehand and mixing will be a lot simpler . . . and a lot faster too.

HOW MUCH WHISKEY SHOULD YOU BUY?

One fifth of Calvert Extra whiskey makes 17 of any of these popular drinks, using 1½ oz. per drink.

Highballs	Whiskey On The Rocks	Old Fashioneds
Whiskey Sours	Mint Juleps	Whiskey Collins
	Manhattans	

One fifth of Calvert Gin makes 17 of any of these popular drinks, using 1½ oz. per drink.

Martinis	Gin Rickeys and Gin Fizzes	Gibsons
Gin 'N' Tonics	Tom Collins	Gin On The Rocks

If You're Having	For Pre-Dinner Cocktails, You'll Average	For A Party, You'll Average
4 people	8 to 12 drinks (one fifth required)	12 to 16 drinks (two fifths required)
6 to 8 people	12 to 24 drinks (two fifths required)	18 to 32 drinks (two fifths required)
12 people	24 to 36 drinks (three fifths required)	36 to 48 drinks (three fifths required)
20 people	40 to 60 drinks (four fifths required)	60 to 80 drinks (five fifths required)
25 people	50 to 75 drinks (five fifths required)	75 to 100 drinks (seventh fifths required)
40 people	80 to 120 drinks (eight fifths required)	120 to 160 drinks (ten fifths required)

Goof-proof Cocktails: For perfect cocktails everytime, stock your bar with Calvert Prepared Cocktails. You'll find the Calvert Martini, Calvert Manhattan, Calvert Whiskey Sour, Calvert Daiquiri, and Calvert Margarita Cocktails at your favorite retailer. They're a cinch to serve. Calvert Cocktails are delicious and wonderfully convenient for parties, when guests drop in, or just for yourself.

CHAPTER TWO

242 VARIOUS PLEASURES OF THE GLASS

HOW TO MIX EVERYBODY'S FAVORITE DRINK

Variety is the spice of parties. Just as your guests will enjoy spending the evening with old friends — they will also welcome the opportunity to meet new people in an atmosphere of good cheer created by drinks that may be old favorites or taste-tempting new ones. As a good all-around host or hostess, you'll be ready to provide both.

Of course, your guest list will take care of the personalities. The following pages of The Calvert Party Encyclopedia will furnish you with the full range of mixed drinks. You're sure to find the perfect mix for every taste — every time — every party.

FOUR ALL-TIME FAVORITES

WHISKEY HIGHBALL

1½ Oz. Calvert Extra

Pour Calvert Extra over ice cubes in highball glass. Fill with favorite mix. Stir gently.

WHISKEY SOUR

1½ Oz. Calvert Extra

Juice of ½ Lemon

½ Teaspoon Sugar

Pour ingredients in shaker with ice. Shake well. Strain. Serve in sour glass. Garnish with cherry and orange slice.

OLD FASHIONED

2 Oz. Calvert Extra

1 Small lump Sugar

1 Dash Bitters

Muddle sugar in Old Fashioned glass with spoonful of water. Add ice, bitters, Calvert Extra. Garnish with cherry, orange slice, and twist of lemon peel as desired. A splash of soda may be added.

MANHATTAN

1½ Oz. Calvert Extra

½ Oz. Sweet Vermouth

1 Dash Bitters

Stir well with ice. Strain into cocktail glass. Serve with cherry.

WHISKEY DRINKS

APPETIZER

2 Oz. Calvert Extra
3 Dashes Curacao
2 Dashes Bitters
1 Twist Lemon Peel
1 Twist Orange Peel
Shake well over ice. Strain into cocktail glass.

ARTIST'S SPECIAL

1 Oz. Calvert Extra
1 Oz. Sherry
½ Oz. Lemon Juice
½ Oz. Sugar Syrup
Stir well with ice. Strain into cocktail glass.

BITTERSWEET

1½ Oz. Calvert Extra
Juice 1 Orange
½ Teaspoon Fine
    Granulated Sugar
2 Dashes Bitters
Shake well with ice. Strain into cocktail glass.

BLINKER

1½ Oz. Calvert Extra
2½ Oz. Grapefruit
    Juice
½ Oz. Grenadine
Shake well with ice. Strain into Old Fashioned glass.

BOILERMAKER

1½ Oz. Calvert Extra
Serve Calvert Extra in jigger with glass of beer on the side.

BRAINSTORM

2 Oz. Calvert Extra
2 Dashes Dry Vermouth
2 Dashes Claristine or
    Benedictine
1 Twist Orange Peel
Pour ingredients in Old Fashioned glass over ice cubes and stir.

BROOKLYN

2 Oz. Calvert Extra
1 Oz. Dry Vermouth
1 Dash Maraschino
1 Dash Bitters
Stir well with ice. Strain into cocktail glass.

CABLEGRAM

2 Oz. Calvert Extra
1 Teaspoon Powdered
    Sugar
Juice of ½ Lemon
Stir well with ice. Strain into 4 Oz. cocktail glass. Fill with ginger ale.

CALVERT 'N' COLA

1½ Oz. Calvert Extra
6 Oz. Cola
4 Dashes Bitters
Serve in highball glass over ice cubes. Stir slightly.

CAPETOWN

1 Oz. Calvert Extra
1 Oz. Dry Vermouth
3 Dashes Curacao
1 Dash Bitters
Stir well with ice. Strain into cocktail glass. Serve with twist of lemon peel.

COMMODORE

2 Oz. Calvert Extra
Juice of ½ Lime or
    Juice of ¼ Lemon
2 Dashes Orange
    Bitters
1 Teaspoon Sugar Syrup
Shake well with ice. Strain
into cocktail glass.

COWBOY

2 Oz. Calvert Extra
1 Oz. Cream
Shake with shaved ice.
Strain into cocktail glass.

CREOLE

1 Oz. Calvert Extra
1 Oz. Sweet Vermouth
2 Dashes Claristine or
    Benedictine
2 Dashes Bitters
Stir with ice. Strain into
cocktail glass. Serve with
twist of lemon peel.

CROWN

2 Oz. Calvert Extra
1 Oz. Lemon Juice
1 Dash Grenadine
Stir well with ice. Strain
into cocktail glass.

DANDY

1 Oz. Calvert Extra
1 Oz. Dry Vermouth
1 Dash Bitters
3 Dashes Triple Sec
1 Twist each Lemon
    and Orange Peel
Stir well with ice. Strain
into cocktail glass.

DERBY

1½ Oz. Calvert Extra
½ Oz. Sweet Vermouth
½ Oz. Curacao
Juice of ½ Lime
Shake well with ice. Strain
into cocktail glass. Garnish
with mint leaf.

DE RIGUEUR

2 Oz. Calvert Extra
1 Oz. Grapefruit Juice
1 Teaspoon Honey
Shake well with ice. Strain
into cocktail glass.

DOWN THE HATCH

1½ Oz. Calvert Extra

3 Dashes Blackberry
    Brandy

2 Dashes Orange
    Bitters

Shake with cracked ice.
Strain into cocktail glass.

EARTHQUAKE

1 Oz. Calvert Extra

1 Oz. Calvert Gin

1 Oz. Anesone or Abisante

Shake well with ice. Strain
into cocktail glass.

EGGNOG (For 12)

1 Fifth Calvert Extra

8 Eggs, Separated

½ Pound Sugar

1 Pint Heavy Cream

1 Quart Milk

3 Oz. Rum — optional

Beat yolks and white separately, adding sugar to
whites. Add Calvert Extra to
yolks, then combine with
rum, heavy cream and milk.
Fold in whites gently. Chill
thoroughly. Serve in cup or
mug. Top with grated nut-
meg.

ELK'S OWN

1 Oz. Calvert Extra

1 Oz. Port

1 Egg White

Juice of ½ Lemon

1 Teaspoon Sugar

Shake well with ice. Strain
into Old Fashioned glass.
Serve with small wedge of
pineapple.

EVERYTHING BUT

1 Oz. Calvert Extra

1 Oz. Calvert Gin

1 Oz. Lemon Juice

1 Oz. Orange Juice

1 Egg

1 Teaspoon Apricot
    Brandy

½ Teaspoon Powdered
    Sugar

Shake well with ice. Strain
into sour glass.

FANCY-FREE FROSTED COCKTAIL

1½ Oz. Calvert Extra

2 Dashes Grenadine

1 Dash Orange Bitters

1 Dash Aromatic Bitters

Dip rim of cocktail glass in
lemon juice. Then dip into
powdered sugar. Shake in-
gredients well with ice.
Strain into prepared glass.

FLU

2 Oz. Calvert Extra

1 Teaspoon Ginger
    Brandy

1 Teaspoon Rock
    Candy Syrup

1 Teaspoon Light Rum

Juice of ¼ Lemon

Stir well without ice. Strain
into cocktail glass.

FOX RIVER

3 Oz. Calvert Extra

1 Oz. Creme de Cacao

4 Dashes Peach Bitters

Stir gently with little ice.
Strain into cocktail glass.
Squeeze lemon peel over
top.

HORSE'S NECK (Spiked)

1½ Oz. Calvert Extra
1 Lemon
Ginger Ale

Remove lemon peel in one long spiral piece, if possible; drape one end over edge of tall highball glass. Add ice and Calvert Extra. Fill with ginger ale.

HOT DECK

3 Oz. Calvert Extra
1 Oz. Sweet Vermouth
1 Dash Jamaica Ginger

Shake well with ice. Strain into cocktail glass.

HOT TODDY

1½ Oz. Calvert Extra
1 Teaspoon Sugar
Small Stick of Cinnamon
Slice of Lemon
4 Cloves

Fill mug ⅔ full of boiling water. Add sugar, cinnamon stick, lemon slice studded with cloves, Calvert Extra. Stir. Serve with a spoon.

HURRICANE

1 Oz. Calvert Extra
1 Oz. Calvert Gin
1 Oz. White Creme
   de Menthe
Juice of 1 Lemon

Shake well with ice. Strain into cocktail glass.

INK STREET

2 Oz. Calvert Extra
1 Oz. Orange Juice
1 Oz. Lemon Juice

Shake well with ice. Strain into cocktail glass.

KLONDIKE COOLER

2 Oz. Calvert Extra
Rind of 1 Orange
Juice of 1 Orange
Ginger Ale

Place ice cubes and whole orange rind in highball glass. Add orange juice, Calvert Extra. Stir. Fill with ginger ale.

LADIES' COCKTAIL

1½ Oz. Calvert Extra
2 Dashes Abisante
   or Anesone
3 Dashes Anisette
1 Dash Bitters

Stir well with ice. Strain into cocktail glass. Serve with piece of pineapple on top.

MASTER OF THE HOUNDS

1½ Oz. Calvert Extra
½ Oz. Cherry Brandy
2 Dashes Bitters

Stir well with ice. Strain into cocktail glass.

19

MILK PUNCH

1½ Oz. Calvert Extra
1 Teaspoon Fine
   Granulated Sugar
4 Oz. Milk

Shake Calvert Extra and milk with ice. Strain into highball glass. Dust nutmeg on top.

MILLIONAIRE COCKTAIL

3 Oz. Calvert Extra
½ Oz. Curacao
Dash Grenadine
White of 1 Egg

Shake well with ice. Strain into cocktail glass.

MINT JULEP

3 Oz. Calvert Extra
4 Sprigs Fresh Mint
1 Small lump sugar

Crush 2 sprigs mint in julep or large highball glass. Rub all over inside then discard mint. Fill glass with crushed ice. Add Calvert Extra and ½ Oz. water in which sugar has been dissolved. Do not stir. Garnish with remaining fresh mint. Arguments over variations are endless. This one is based on Irvin S. Cobb's recipe.

MINT SMASH

1½ Oz. Calvert Extra
2 Sprigs Fresh Mint
1 Teaspoon Sugar
Soda

Crush mint and sugar in highball glass with a few drops of water. Add half a glass of shaved ice, Calvert Extra and fill with soda. Decorate with mint.

MONTE CARLO COCKTAIL

1½ Oz. Calvert Extra
½ Oz. Claristine or
   Benedictine
2 Dashes Bitters

Shake well with ice. Strain into cocktail glass.

MORNING GLORY FIZZ

1½ Oz. Calvert Extra
1 Oz. Bitters
Juice of ½ Lime
½ Oz. Abisante or
   Anesone
White of 1 Egg
½ Teaspoon Fine
   Granulated Sugar

Shake well with ice. Strain into a highball glass. Fill with soda and stir lightly.

NEW YORK COCKTAIL

1½ Oz. Calvert Extra
½ Teaspoon Powdered
   Sugar
1 Dash Grenadine
Juice of ½ Lime

Shake well with ice. Strain into cocktail glass. Decorate with twist of orange peel.

OPENING

2 Oz. Calvert Extra
1 Oz. Sweet Vermouth
½ Oz. Grenadine

Stir well with ice. Strain into cocktail glass.

PADDY

1 Oz. Calvert Extra
1 Oz. Sweet Vermouth
1 Dash Bitters

Stir well with ice. Strain into cocktail glass.

PALMER COCKTAIL

1½ Oz. Calvert Extra
1 Dash Bitters
1 Dash Lemon Juice

Stir well with ice. Strain into cocktail glass.

SARATOGA FIZZ

1½ Oz. Calvert Extra
½ Oz. Lemon Juice
1 Teaspoon Lime Juice
1 Teaspoon Sugar
1 Egg White

Shake well with ice. Strain into cocktail glass. Garnish with cherry.

SAZERAC

2 Oz. Calvert Extra
2 Dashes Anesone or
   Abisante
2 Dashes Bitters
1 Lump Sugar,
   dissolved in
   1 teaspoon water

Stir well with ice. Strain into chilled cocktail glass. Twist lemon peel over top.

SOUVENIR

1 Oz. Calvert Extra
1 Oz. Dry Vermouth
1 Orange Slice
1 Slice Orange

Stir well with ice. Strain into cocktail glass.

T. N.T.

1 Oz. Calvert Extra
1 Oz. Anesone or
   Abisante

Shake well with ice. Strain into cocktail glass.

TEMPTATION

1½ Oz. Calvert Extra
2 Dashes Curacao
2 Dashes Anesone or
   Abisante
2 Dashes Dry
   Vermouth

Stir well with ice. Strain into cocktail glass. Decorate with twists of orange and lemon peel.

TOM 'N' JERRY

2 Oz. Calvert Extra

1 Egg, Separated

1 Teaspoon Sugar

Hot Water or Milk

Beat yolk and white separately, adding sugar to yolk. Mix. Put two tablespoonsful of batter in large mug. Add Calvert Extra. Fill with hot water or milk. Top with grated nutmeg. Brandy or rum may be added.

UP-TO-DATE

1 Oz. Calvert Extra

1 Oz. Sherry

3 Dashes Bitters

2 Dashes Triple Sec

Stir well with ice. Strain into cocktail glass.

WALDORF COCKTAIL

1 Oz. Calvert Extra

1 Oz. Abisante or
  Anesone

1 Oz. Sweet Vermouth

3 Dashes Bitters

Stir well with ice. Strain into cocktail glass.

WARD EIGHT

1½ Oz. Calvert Extra

3 Dashes Grenadine

¾ Oz. Lemon Juice

Sugar as desired

Shake well with ice. Strain into highball glass or goblet. Add slice of orange and a cherry. Top with soda, if desired.

WHISKEY 'N' BITTERS

1½ Oz. Calvert Extra

2 Dashes Bitters

Pour over ice cubes into oversize whiskey glass. Stir well before serving.

WHISKEY COLLINS

1½ Oz. Calvert Extra

Juice of ½ Lime

Stir with ice. Strain into highball glass. Fill with club soda.

WHISKEY FLIP

2 Oz. Calvert Extra

1 Egg

1 Teaspoon Powdered
  Sugar

Shake well with cracked ice. Strain into cocktail glass. Sprinkle nutmeg on top.

WHISKEY LEMONADE
(Serves 4 to 6)

8 Oz. Calvert Extra

Juice of 6 Lemons

1 Quart Water

1 Cup Sugar Syrup

Combine in pitcher and chill. Pour over ice cubes in highball glasses. Garnish with fruit or mint as desired.

WHISKEY ON THE ROCKS

2 Oz. Calvert Extra

Pour over ice in Old Fashioned glass.

FOUR ALL-TIME FAVORITES

GIN 'N' TONIC

    1½ Oz. Calvert Gin
    Lime
    Tonic

Pour Calvert Gin over ice in highball glass. Add slice or half of lime. Fill with quinine water.

TOM COLLINS

    1½ Oz. Calvert Gin
    Juice of ½ Lemon
    1 Teapoon Sugar

Mix lemon and sugar in highball glass. Add ice and Calvert Gin. Stir well. Add soda, cherry, slice of orange.

100% DRY MARTINI

    2 Oz. Calvert Gin
    ½ Oz. Dry Vermouth

Stir with ice and strain into chilled cocktail glass. Serve with twist of lemon peel or olive.

GIN RICKEY

    1½ Oz. Calvert Gin
    Juice of ½ Lime

Pour over ice cubes in highball glass. Drop in lime rind. Fill with soda.

GIN DRINKS

ABBEY COCKTAIL

2 Oz. Calvert Gin
1 Teaspoon Sweet
Vermouth
1 Oz. Orange Juice
2 Dashes Bitters

Stir well with ice. Strain into cocktail glass. Serve with a twist of orange peel or cherry.

ALASKA COCKTAIL

3 Oz. Calvert Gin
1 Oz. Yellow
Chartreuse
2 Dashes Orange
Bitters

Stir well with ice. Strain into cocktail glass. Serve with a twist of lemon peel.

ALFONSO SPECIAL

1 Oz. Calvert Gin
1 Oz. Dry Vermouth
2 Oz. Curacao
4 Dashes Sweet
Vermouth
1 Dash Bitters

Shake well with ice. Strain into cocktail glass.

ALLIES

1 Oz. Calvert Gin
1 Oz. Dry Vermouth
2 Dashes Kummel

Stir well with ice. Strain into cocktail glass.

ANGEL FACE

1 Oz. Calvert Gin
1 Oz. Apricot Brandy
1 Oz. Calvados or
Apple Brandy

Stir well with ice. Strain into cocktail glass.

ANNIVERSARY COCKTAIL

1 Oz. Calvert Gin
1 Oz. Brandy
2 Dashes Orange
Bitters

Shake well with cracked ice. Strain into cocktail glass.

AROUND THE WORLD COCKTAIL

1 Oz. Calvert Gin
1 Oz. Green Creme de
Menthe
1 Oz. Pineapple Juice

Shake well with cracked ice. Strain into cocktail glass.

ARTILLERY

2 Oz. Calvert Gin
1 Oz. Sweet Vermouth
2 Dashes Bitters

Stir well with ice. Strain into cocktail glass. Serve with a twist of lemon peel.

ASTORIA

2 Oz. Calvert Gin
1 Oz. Dry Vermouth
1 Dash Orange Bitters

Stir well with ice. Strain into cocktail glass. Serve with olive.

ATTENTION

1 Oz. Calvert Gin
1 Oz. Ansone or
    Abisante
1 Oz. Dry Vermouth
1 Oz. Creme de Noya
2 Dashes Orange
    Bitters

Stir well with ice. Strain into Old Fashioned glass.

B.V.D.

1 Oz. Calvert Gin
1 Oz. Light Rum
1 Oz. Dry Vermouth

Stir well with ice. Strain into cocktail glass.

BARBARY COAST

1 Oz. Calvert Gin
1 Oz. Scotch
1 Oz. Creme de Cacao
1 Oz. Cream

Shake well with ice. Strain into Old Fashioned glass.

BARKING DOG

1 Oz. Calvert Gin
1 Oz. Dry Vermouth
1 Oz. Sweet Vermouth
2 Dashes Bitters

Stir well with ice. Strain into cocktail glass. Serve with cherry.

BARNUM

2 Oz. Calvert Gin
1 Oz. Apricot Brandy
2 Dashes Bitters
1 Dash Lemon or Lime
    Juice

Shake well with ice. Strain into cocktail glass.

BEES' KNEES

1½ Oz. Calvert Gin
1 Teaspoon Honey
Juice of ¼ Lemon

Shake well with ice. Strain into cocktail glass.

BIJOU COCKTAIL

1 Oz. Calvert Gin
1 Oz. Green
    Chartreuse
1 Oz. Sweet Vermouth
1 Dash Orange Bitters

Stir well with ice. Strain into cocktail glass. Serve with a twist of lemon peel.

BLUE DEVIL

2 Oz. Calvert Gin
1 Oz. Maraschino
1 Oz. Lemon or Lime
    Juice
1 Dash Blue Vegetable
    Extract (coloring)

Shake well with ice. Strain into cocktail glass.

BON APPETIT

2 Oz. Calvert Gin
½ Oz. Dry Vermouth
½ Oz. Sweet Vermouth
3 Dashes Bitters
Juice of ½ Orange

Shake well with ice. Strain into cocktail glass.

BRONX (Dry)

3 Oz. Calvert Gin
1 Oz. Dry Vermouth
Juice of ¼ Orange

Stir well with ice. Strain into cocktail glass.

BRONX (Sweet)

2 Oz. Calvert Gin
1 Oz. Dry Vermouth
1 Oz. Sweet Vermouth
Juice of ¼ Orange

Stir well with ice. Strain into cocktail glass.

BROOKLYN (GIN)

2 Oz. Calvert Gin
1 Oz. Sweet Vermouth
2 Dashes Orange Juice
½ Egg White
Nutmeg

Shake with ice. Strain into cocktail glass. Add grated nutmeg.

BULLDOG

2 Oz. Calvert Gin
Juice of 1 Orange
Ginger Ale

Stir Calvert Gin and orange juice with ice in large Old Fashioned glass. Fill with ginger ale.

BUNNY HUG

1 Oz. Calvert Gin
1 Oz. Calvert Extra
1 Oz. Abisante or
  Anesone

Shake well with ice. Strain into cocktail glass.

CLARIDGE

1 Oz. Calvert Gin
1 Oz. Dry Vermouth
1 Oz. Apricot Brandy
1 Dash Triple Sec

Stir well with ice. Strain into cocktail glass. Serve with cherry.

CLOVER CLUB

2 Oz. Calvert Gin
4 Dashes Grenadine
Juice of ½ Lemon
1 Egg White

Shake well with ice. Strain into cocktail glass.

COLONIAL

2 Oz. Calvert Gin
1 Oz. Grapefruit Juice
3 Dashes Maraschino

Shake well with ice. Strain into cocktail glass.

CORNELL COCKTAIL

1½ Oz. Calvert Gin

3 Dashes Maraschino

1 Egg White

Shake well with ice. Strain into cocktail glass.

DAMN THE WEATHER

2 Oz. Calvert Gin

1 Oz. Sweet Vermouth

1 Oz. Orange Juice

3 Dashes Curacao

Shake well with ice. Strain into cocktail glass.

DARBY

1½ Oz. Calvert Gin

½ Oz. Lime Juice

½ Oz. Grapefruit Juice

1 Teaspoon Powdered Sugar

Shake well with ice. Strain into cocktail glass. Top with dash of soda. Add cherry.

DIXIE

2 Oz. Calvert Gin

1 Oz. Anesone or Abisante

1 Oz. Dry Vermouth

Juice of ¼ Orange

2 Dashes Grenadine

Shake well with ice. Strain into cocktail glass.

ECLIPSE

2 Oz. Calvert Gin

Grenadine

Place cherry or ripe olive in a cocktail glass. Add grenadine to cover. Shake the gin with ice. Strain slowly into glass so as not to mix with grenadine. Twist an orange peel over top.

FALLEN ANGEL

2 Oz. Calvert Gin

Juice of 1 Lemon or Lime

2 Dashes Creme de Menthe

1 Dash Bitters

Stir well with ice. Strain into cocktail glass. Serve with cherry.

FARE-THE-WELL

2 Oz. Calvert Gin

1 Oz. Dry Vermouth

2 Dashes Sweet Vermouth

6 Dashes Curacao

Shake well with ice. Strain into cocktail glass.

FRENCH "75"

2 Oz. Calvert Gin

1 Oz. Lemon Juice

1 Teaspoon Powdered Sugar

Champagne

Pour into highball glass over cracked ice. Stir. Fill with Champagne.

GIBSON

2 Oz. Calvert Gin

½ Oz. Dry Vermouth

Stir with ice. Strain into cocktail glass. Serve with pearl onion.

GIMLET

2 Oz. Calvert Gin

¾ Oz. Lime Juice

Stir or shake with ice and serve in cocktail glass.

GIN BUCK

1½ Oz. Calvert Gin

Juice of ½ Lime

Squeeze lime into highball glass. Add lime peel, ice, then gin. Fill with ginger ale. Stir slightly.

GIN DAISY

1½ Oz. Calvert Gin

4 Dashes Grenadine

1 Oz. Lemon Juice

Pour into mixing glass. Add finely cracked ice. Shake well. Pour unstrained into highball glass. Decorate with fruit.

GIN FIZZ

1½ Oz. Calvert Gin

1 Oz. Fresh Lemon Juice

1 Teaspoon Fine Granulated Sugar

Shake well with cracked ice. Strain into highball glass. Fill with soda. Stir slightly.

GIN SLING

1½ Oz. Calvert Gin

3 Dashes Bitters — optional

Twist of Lemon Peel

Pour in highball glass over cracked ice. Add soda. Stir.

GIN SOUR

1½ Oz. Calvert Gin

½ Teaspoon Sugar

Juice of ½ Lemon

Shake well with ice. Serve in sour glass. Garnish with cherry and orange slice.

GIN STINGER

2 Oz. Calvert Gin

1 Oz. White Creme de Menthe

Shake well with shaved ice. Strain into cocktail glass.

GIN SWIZZLE

1½ Oz. Calvert Gin

¾ Oz. Fresh Lime Juice

1 Teaspoon Fine Granulated Sugar

6 Dashes Bitters — optional

Pour ingredients into pitcher. Add shaved ice. Mix vigorously until the pitcher begins to frost. Then strain into cocktail glass and serve. Or serve with cracked ice in tall glass.

GIN 'N' BITTERS

2 Oz. Calvert Gin

1 Dash Angostura Bitters

Pour over ice in Old Fashioned glass and serve.

GIN 'N' SODA

2 Oz. Calvert Gin

Soda

Pour Calvert Gin into highball glass full of ice. Fill with soda. Stir once.

GIN ON THE ROCKS

2 Oz. Calvert Gin

Pour over ice cubes in Old Fashioned glass. Add twist of lemon peel.

GUNGA DIN

3 Oz. Calvert Gin

1 Oz. Dry Vermouth

1 Slice Pineapple

Juice of ¼ Orange

Shake well with ice. Strain into Old Fashioned glass.

HAWAIIAN NO. 1

1½ Oz. Calvert Gin

¾ Oz. Pineapple Juice

1 Dash Orange Bitters

1 Egg White

Shake well with ice. Strain into cocktail glass.

HAWAIIAN NO. 2

2 Oz. Calvert Gin

½ Oz. Orange Juice

½ Oz. Curacao

Shake well with ice. Strain into cocktail glass.

HONOLULU LULU

1 Oz. Calvert Gin

1 Oz. Claristine or Benedictine

1 Oz. Maraschino

Stir well with ice. Strain into cocktail glass.

IDEAL

2 Oz. Calvert Gin

1 Oz. Sweet Vermouth

3 Dashes Maraschino

1 Tablespoon Grapefruit Juice

Shake well with ice. Strain into cocktail glass.

JAVA COOLER

1½ Oz. Calvert Gin

Juice of ½ Lime

3 Dashes Bitters

Quinine Water

Place ice cubes in highball glass. Add juice of ½ lime, bitters and Calvert Gin. Fill glass with quinine water. Stir slightly.

KNOCKOUT

1 Oz. Calvert Gin

1 Oz. Dry Vermouth

1 Oz. Anesone or Abisante

1 Teaspoon White Creme de Menthe — optional

Stir well with ice. Strain into sour glass. Serve with mint leaves.

LEO SPECIAL

2 Oz. Calvert Gin

1 Oz. Lime Juice

1 Oz. Triple Sec

2 Dashes Anesone or Abisante

Stir well with ice. Strain into cocktail glass.

29

MAIDEN'S BLUSH

2 Oz. Calvert Gin
4 Dashes Curacao
4 Dashes Grenadine
2 Dashes Lemon Juice

Shake well with ice. Strain into cocktail glass.

MAIDEN'S PRAYER

1½ Oz. Calvert Gin
1½ Oz. Triple Sec
½ Oz. Lemon Juice
½ Teaspoon Orange Juice

Stir well with ice. Strain into cocktail glass.

MAURICE

1½ Oz. Calvert Gin
¾ Oz. Sweet Vermouth
¾ Oz. Dry Vermouth
Juice of ¼ Orange
1 Dash Bitters

Stir well with ice. Strain into cocktail glass.

MINNEHAHA

2 Oz. Calvert Gin
1 Oz. Dry Vermouth
1 Oz. Sweet Vermouth
Juice of ¼ Orange

Shake well with ice. Strain into cocktail glass.

NEWBURY

1 Oz. Calvert Gin
1 Oz. Sweet Vermouth
3 Dashes Curacao
1 Twist Lemon Peel
1 Twist Orange Peel

Stir well with ice. Strain into cocktail glass.

NIGHTMARE

1 Oz. Calvert Gin
½ Oz. Dry Vermouth
½ Oz. Cherry Brandy
½ Oz. Orange Juice

Shake well with ice. Strain into cocktail glass.

ONE EXCITING NIGHT

1 Oz. Calvert Gin
¾ Oz. Dry Vermouth
¾ Oz. Sweet Vermouth
1 Dash Orange Juice

Frost glass by first dipping rim in lemon juice, and then into powdered sugar. Shake ingredients well with ice. Strain into cocktail glass. Add twist of lemon peel.

ORANGE BLOSSOM

2 Oz. Calvert Gin
1 Oz. Orange Juice

Stir well with cracked ice and strain into cocktail glass.

PALISADES COCKTAIL

1 Oz. Calvert Gin
1 Oz. Cider
2 Dashes Bitters

Shake well with cracked ice.
Strain into cocktail glass.

PARADISE COCKTAIL

1 Oz. Calvert Gin
1 Oz. Apricot Brandy
1 Oz. Orange or
    Lemon Juice

Stir well with ice. Strain into
cocktail glass.

PINK BABY

2 Oz. Calvert Gin
½ Oz. Grenadine
½ Oz. Lemon Juice
1 Egg White

Shake well with ice. Strain
into cocktail glass.

PINK LADY

2 Oz. Calvert Gin
½ Oz. Apple Brandy —
    optional
½ Oz. Lemon Juice
½ Oz. Grenadine
1 Egg White

Shake well with ice. Strain
into cocktail glass.

POLLYANNA

1½ Oz. Calvert Gin
½ Oz. Grenadine
½ Oz. Sweet Vermouth
3 Slices Orange
3 Slices Pineapple

Muddle orange and pine-
apple slices in bottom of
shaker. Add ice and other
ingredients. Shake well.
Strain into cocktail glass.

PRINCETON COCKTAIL

1½ Oz. Calvert Gin
½ Oz. Port — optional
2 Dashes Orange
    Bitters

Stir with ice. Strain into
cocktail glass. Serve with a
twist of lemon peel.

RAMOS FIZZ

1½ Oz. Calvert Gin
Juice of ½ Lemon
Juice of ½ Lime
1 Oz. Cream
½ Teaspoon Sugar
White of 1 Egg

Shake with crushed ice vigorously and at length. Strain
into small highball glass.

SALOME

1 Oz. Calvert Gin
1 Oz. Dry Vermouth
1 Tablespoon Sweet
    Vermouth

Stir well with ice. Strain into
cocktail glass.

31

SAVOY SPECIAL

1½ Oz. Calvert Gin

1 Oz. Dry Vermouth

2 Dashes Grenadine

1 Dash Anesone or
    Abisante

Stir well with ice. Strain into cocktail glass. Add lemon peel.

SEVENTH HEAVEN

1 Oz. Calvert Gin

1 Oz. Sweet Vermouth

2 Dashes Maraschino

1 Dash Bitters

Stir well with ice. Strain into cocktail glass. Add orange peel, cherry.

SILVER KING

1½ Oz. Calvert Gin

Juice of ½ Lemon

2 Dashes Orange Bitters

2 Dashes Sugar Syrup

1 Egg White

Shake well with ice. Strain into cocktail glass.

SNOWBALL

1½ Oz. Calvert Gin

½ Oz. White Creme
    de Menthe

½ Oz. Anisette

½ Oz. Cream

Shake well with ice. Strain into cocktail glass.

SOUTHSIDE

2 Oz. Calvert Gin

Juice of ½ Lemon

½ Tablespoon Sugar

2 Sprigs of Fresh Mint

Shake well with ice and strain into cocktail glass. Add a dash of soda.

STUBBY COLLINS

2 Oz. Calvert Gin

1 Oz. Lemon Juice

1 Teaspoon Fine
    Granulated Sugar

Stir well with ice. Serve in Old Fashioned glass.

TANGO

1½ Oz. Calvert Gin

¾ Oz. Sweet Vermouth

¾ Oz. Dry Vermouth

2 Dashes Curacao

Juice of ¼ Orange

Stir well with ice. Strain into cocktail glass.

TURF

1½ Oz. Calvert Gin

¾ Oz. Dry Vermouth

2 Dashes Anisette

2 Dashes Maraschino

2 Dashes Bitters

Shake with ice, strain into cocktail glass.

TUXEDO

1½ Oz. Calvert Gin

½ Oz. Medium Dry
    Sherry

1 Dash Bitters

Stir vigorously with ice. Strain into chilled cocktail glass.

YALE

1½ Oz. Calvert Gin

½ Oz. Dry Vermouth

3 Dashes Orange
    Bitters

2 Dashes Sugar Syrup

1 Dash Maraschino

Stir well with ice. Strain into cocktail glass.

FOUR ALL-TIME FAVORITES

SCOTCH SOUR

1½ Oz. Scotch
Juice of ½ Lemon
½ Teaspoon Sugar

Shake well with ice. Serve in sour glass. Garnish with cherry and orange slices.

SCOTCH ON THE ROCKS

2 Oz. Scotch

Pour over ice in Old Fashioned glass. Splash of soda and twist of lemon peel are optional accessories.

SCOTCH 'N' SODA

1½ Oz. Scotch

Pour over ice cubes in highball glass. Fill with soda. Stir.

ROB ROY

1½ Oz. Scotch
1 Oz. Sweet Vermouth
2 Dashes Bitters

Stir well with ice. Strain into cocktail glass. Serve with twist of lemon peel.

SCOTCH DRINKS

AFFINITY COCKTAIL

1 Oz. Scotch
¾ Oz. Dry Vermouth
¾ Oz. Sweet Vermouth
2 Dashes Bitters

Stir well with ice. Strain into cocktail glass. Serve with cherry and twist of lemon peel.

ALICE COCKTAIL

1 Oz. Scotch
¾ Oz. Kummel
¾ Oz. Sweet Vermouth

Stir well with ice. Strain into cocktail glass.

BLOOD AND SAND

1 Oz. Scotch
¾ Oz. Cherry Brandy
¾ Oz. Sweet Vermouth
¾ Oz. Orange Juice

Stir well with ice. Strain into cocktail glass.

BOBBY BURNS

1 Oz. Scotch
1 Oz. Dry Vermouth
1 Oz. Sweet Vermouth
1 Dash Claristine or
    Benedictine

Stir well with ice. Strain into cocktail glass.

FLYING SCOTCHMAN

1 Oz. Scotch
½ Oz. Italian Vermouth
1 Dash Bitters
1 Dash Sugar Syrup

Shake with cracked ice. Strain into cocktail glass.

HIGHLAND FLING

1½ Oz. Scotch
1 Teaspoon Sugar
2 Oz. Milk

Shake well with ice. Strain into sour glass. Sprinkle nutmeg on top.

LOCH LOMOND

1½ Oz. Scotch
3 Dashes Bitters
1 Teaspoon Sugar

Shake well with ice. Serve in Old Fashioned glass.

MAMIE TAYLOR

1½ Oz. Scotch
Juice of ½ Lime
Ginger Ale

Squeeze lime into highball glass. Add ice cubes, Scotch. Fill with ginger ale.

MICKEY WALKER

2 Oz. Scotch
1 Oz. Sweet Vermouth
I Dash Lemon Juice
1 Dash Grenadine

Shake well with ice. Strain into cocktail glass.

SCOTCH MIST

2 Oz. Scotch

1 Twist Lemon Peel

Shaved Ice

Fill Old Fashioned glass with shaved ice. Pour in Scotch. Add twist of lemon peel.

SCOTCH SIDE CAR

1½ Oz. Scotch

¾ Oz. Triple Sec

¾ Oz. Lemon Juice

Shake well with ice. Strain into cocktail glass.

THISTLE

1 Oz. Scotch

1 Oz. Sweet Vermouth

2 Dashes Bitters

Stir well with ice. Strain into cocktail glass.

TOOTS SHOR

½ Oz. Scotch

½ Oz. Creme de Noya

½ Oz. Italian Vermouth

2 Dashes Anesone

2 Dashes Orange Bitters

Shake with cracked ice. Strain into cocktail glass.

FOUR ALL-TIME FAVORITES

DAIQUIRI

2 Oz. Light Rum
Juice of ½ Lime
1 Teaspoon Sugar

Shake with ice. Pour into cocktail glass.

RUM COLLINS

2 Oz. Light Rum
Juice of ½ Lemon
1 Teaspoon Sugar

Pour Rum in highball glass over ice. Stir well. Add soda, cherry, slice of orange.

RUM 'N' COLA (Cuba Libre)

1½ Oz. Light Rum
Cola

Pour rum over ice in tall glass. Add cola as desired. Stir once.

PLANTER'S PUNCH

3 Oz. Light Rum
1 Oz. Lime Juice
1 Teaspoon Sugar

Shake Rum, lime juice and sugar. Pour into highball glass over cracked ice. Garnish with cherry and half slices of lemon, orange, slices of pineapple.

RUM DRINKS

AIRMAIL COCKTAIL

1½ Oz. Light Rum
Juice of ½ Lime
1 Teaspoon Honey
Champagne

Shake well with cracked ice. Strain into a highball glass. Fill with Champagne. Stir slightly.

BEE'S KISS

1½ Oz. Light Rum
1 Teaspoon Honey
1 Teaspoon Cream

Shake well with ice. Strain into cocktail glass.

BETWEEN THE SHEETS

½ Oz. Light Rum
½ Oz. Triple Sec
½ Oz. Brandy
½ Oz. Lemon Juice

Shake well with cracked ice. Strain into cocktail glass.

BLACK ROSE

1½ Oz. Rum
1 Teaspoon Sugar
Cold Black Coffee

Combine over ice in highball glass or goblet. Stir and serve.

BOLO

2 Oz. Light Rum
Juice of ½ Lemon or Lime
Juice of ¼ Orange
1 Teaspoon Powdered Sugar

Shake well with ice. Strain into cocktail glass.

CHINESE

1½ Oz. Dark Rum
1½ Oz. Grenadine
3 Dashes Curacao
3 Dashes Maraschino
1 Dash Bitters

Stir well with ice. Strain into cocktail glass. Serve with cherry.

COLUMBIA COCKTAIL

1½ Oz. Light Rum
½ Oz. Raspberry Syrup
⅓ Oz. Lemon Juice

Shake well with ice. Strain into cocktail glass.

COUNTRY LIFE

1 Oz. Dark Rum
2 Oz. Calvert Extra
3 Dashes Bitters
1 Dash Orange Bitters

Shake well with ice. Strain into cocktail glass.

EL PRESIDENTE

1½ Oz. Light Rum
½ Oz. Curacao
½ Oz. Dry Vermouth
1 Dash Grenadine

Shake well with ice. Strain into cocktail glass.

FIREMAN'S SOUR

2 Oz. Light Rum
½ Teaspoon Powdered
Sugar
Juice of 1 Lime
½ Oz. Grenadine

Shake well with ice. Strain into sour glass. Decorate with orange and lime slices.

FLORIDA SPECIAL

1½ Oz. Light Rum
1 Teaspoon Dry
Vermouth
1 Teaspoon Sweet
Vermouth
1 Oz. Unsweetened
Grapefruit Juice

Stir with shaved ice. Strain into cocktail glass.

FLYING SAUCER

1 Oz. Light Rum
½ Oz. Dry Vermouth
½ Oz. Swedish Punch
1 Dash Grenadine

Shake well with cracked ice. Strain into cocktail glass.

FOX TROT

2 Oz. Light Rum
2 Dashes Curacao
Juice of ½ Lime or
Lemon

Shake well with ice. Strain into cocktail glass.

HAVANA #2

1½ Oz. Light Rum
1 Oz. Pineapple Juice
½ Oz. Lemon Juice

Shake well with ice. Strain into cocktail glass.

HONEYSUCKLE

1½ Oz. Light Rum
1 Teaspoon Honey
Juice of ½ Lime or
Lemon

Shake well with ice. Strain into cocktail glass.

HOT BUTTERED RUM

2 Oz. Dark Rum
1 Twist Lemon Peel
1 Stick Cinnamon
1 or 2 Cloves
Boiling Cider or Water
Butter

Place Rum, lemon peel, cloves and cinnamon in a pewter tankard or heavy mug. Fill with boiling cider or water. Float pat of butter on top and stir well.

JAMAICA GINGER

2 Oz. Dark Rum
1 Oz. Grenadine
3 Dashes Maraschino
3 Dashes Curacao
1 Dash Bitters

Shake well with ice. Strain into cocktail glass.

KINGSTON COCKTAIL

1½ Oz. Dark Rum
1 Oz. Kummel
1 Oz. Orange Juice
1 Dash Bitters

Shake well with ice. Strain into cocktail glass.

LATIN MANHATTAN

1½ Oz. Light Rum
1 Oz. Dry Vermouth
1 Oz. Sweet Vermouth
2 Dashes Bitters

Pour ingredients in mixing glass. Fill with cracked ice. Stir until mixed. Strain into cocktail glass. Add twist of lemon peel and serve.

MIAMI BEACH COCKTAIL

1½ Oz. Light Rum
½ Oz. Triple Sec
1 Dash Lemon or Lime Juice

Shake well with ice. Strain into cocktail glass.

NAKED LADY

1 Oz. Light Rum
1 Oz. Sweet Vermouth
4 Dashes Apricot Brandy
2 Dashes Grenadine
4 Dashes Lemon Juice

Shake well with ice. Strain into cocktail glass.

PARISIAN BLONDE

1 Oz. Dark Rum
1 Oz. Curacao
1 Oz. Cream

Shake well with ice. Strain into cocktail glass.

PIRATE'S PRIZE

2 Oz. Dark Rum
1 Oz. Sweet Vermouth
1 Dash Bitters

Stir well with ice. Strain into cocktail glass.

RUM MANHATTAN

2 Oz. Light Rum
1 Oz. Sweet Vermouth
1 Dash Bitters

Pour ingredients in a mixing glass. Fill with cracked ice. Stir until mixed. Strain and serve in cocktail glass.

RUM OLD FASHIONED

2 Oz. Light Rum
1 Small Lump Sugar
1 Dash Bitters

Muddle sugar in Old Fashioned glass with spoonful of water. Add ice, bitters, Rum. Garnish with cherry, orange slice, and twist of lemon peel as desired. A splash of soda may be added.

RUM SOUR

2 Oz. Rum
Juice of 1 Lime
Sugar to taste

Shake well with shaved ice. Strain into sour glass. Add slice of orange and cherry.

SANTIAGO

2 Oz. Light Rum
2 Dashes Grenadine
4 Dashes Lime Juice

Stir well with ice. Strain into cocktail glass.

SAXON

1½ Oz. Light Rum
2 Dashes Grenadine
1 Twist Orange Peel
Juice of ½ Lime

Shake well with ice. Strain into cocktail glass.

SEPTEMBER MORN

2 Oz. Light Rum
3 Dashes Grenadine
Juice of ½ Lime
1 Egg White

Shake well with ice. Strain into cocktail glass.

SUBURBAN COCKTAIL

1½ Oz. Calvert Extra
¾ Oz. Light Rum
¾ Oz. Port Wine
3 Dashes Bitters
1 Dash Orange Bitters

Shake well with ice. Strain into cocktail glass.

TRINIDAD

1½ Oz. Dark Rum
Juice of ½ Lime
1 Teaspoon Powdered
    Sugar
3 Dashes Bitters

Shake well with ice. Strain into cocktail glass.

WHITE LION

1½ Oz. Dark Rum
Juice of ½ Lemon
1 Teaspoon Powdered
    Sugar
3 Dashes Bitters
3 Dashes Raspberry
    Syrup

Shake well with ice. Strain into cocktail glass.

ZOMBIE

1 Oz. Jamaican Rum
2 Oz. Gold Label Rum
1 Oz. White Label Rum
1 Oz. Pineapple Juice
1 Oz. Papaya Juice
Juice of 1 Lime
1 Teaspoon Powdered
    Sugar

Shake well with ice and pour into 14-ounce highball glass. Decorate with pineapple and cherry. Sprinkle lightly with powdered sugar and serve. Variations are endless.

VODKA DRINKS

BLOODY MARY
1½ Oz. Vodka

3 Oz. Tomato Juice

½ Oz. Lemon Juice

1 Dash Worcestershire
Sauce

Salt and Pepper to taste

Shake well with ice. Strain into highball glass. For a surprising taste treat, use Calvert Gin instead of Vodka.

BLUE MONDAY
2 Oz. Vodka

1 Oz. Triple Sec

1 Dash Blue Vegetable
Extract (coloring)

Stir well with ice. Strain into cocktail glass.

KANGAROO
2 Oz. Vodka

1 Oz. Dry Vermouth

Stir with cracked ice. Strain into cocktail glass. Serve with twist of lemon peel.

MOSCOW MULE
1½ Part Vodka

Ginger Beer

1 Slice Lime

Serve over ice in highball glass, brass or copper mug.

RUSSIAN BEAR
1½ Oz. Vodka

1 Oz. Creme de Cacao

1 Oz. Cream

Stir well with ice. Strain into cocktail glass.

SCREWDRIVER
1 Oz. Vodka

4 Oz. Orange Juice

Pour over ice cubes in highball glass.

TOVARICH
1½ Oz. Vodka

1 Oz. Kummel

Juice of ½ Lime

Shake with cracked ice. Strain into cocktail glass.

41

VODKA MARTINI

2 Oz. Vodka
¾ Oz. Dry Vermouth
Stir well with ice. Strain into cocktail glass. Serve with a twist of lemon peel.

VODKA SLING

2 Oz. Vodka
1 Oz. Cherry Brandy
Juice of ½ Lime

Fill highball glass half full of ice. Place sliced red and green cherries alternately around inside of glass. Add lime and Vodka. Then fill glass with shaved ice. Add Cherry Brandy. Garnish with slice of orange, cherry and peel of cucumber. Serve with straws. Do not stir or shake.

VODKA TWISTER

1½ Oz. Vodka
Lemon Soda
Juice of ½ Lime
Serve with ice in highball glass. Add lime peel.

VOLGA BOATMAN

1 Oz. Vodka
1 Oz. Cherry Brandy
1 Oz. Orange Juice
Stir well with ice. Strain into cocktail glass.

BRANDY DRINKS

APPLE

¾ Oz. Calvert Gin
1½ Oz. Calvados or Applejack
1½ Oz. Apple Cider
¾ Oz. Brandy
Shake with cracked ice. Strain into sour glass.

BALTIMORE BRACER

1 Oz. Brandy
1 Oz. Anisette
1 Egg White
Shake well with ice. Strain into cocktail glass.

BETTER THAN ANYTHING

3 Oz. Brandy
1 Tablespoon Grenadine
1 Tablespoon Curacao
4 Oz. Cherry Brandy
1 Tablespoon Lemon Juice
Shake with cracked ice. Serve in highball glass.

BOMBAY COCKTAIL

1½ Oz. Brandy
¾ Oz. Sweet Vermouth
¾ Oz. Dry Vermouth
2 Dashes Curacao
1 Dash Anesone or
    Abisante

Stir well with ice. Strain into cocktail glass.

BRANDY ALEXANDER

1 Oz. Brandy
¾ Oz. Heavy Cream
¾ Oz. Creme de Cacao

Shake vigorously with cracked ice. Strain into cocktail glass.

BRANDY BLAZER

2 Oz. Brandy
1 Twist Orange Peel
1 Twist Lemon Peel
1 Lump Sugar

Place sugar in bottom of wide-mouth metal glass. Add other ingredients. Stir with long spoon. Ignite with match for a few seconds; then extinguish. Strain into cocktail glass. Serve after dinner.

BRANDY SOUR

1½ Oz. Brandy
Juice of ½ Lemon
1 Teaspoon Sugar

Shake well with ice, strain into sour glass. Add a cherry and twist of lemon peel.

CHAMPS ELYSEES

1 Oz. Cognac
½ Oz. Green
    Chartreuse
1 Teaspoon Lemon
    Juice
2 Drops Bitters

Shake with cracked ice. Strain into cocktail glass.

DEAUVILLE

1 Oz. Brandy
1 Oz. Calvados or
    Apple Brandy
1 Oz. Triple Sec
1 Oz. Lemon Juice

Stir well with ice. Strain into sour glass.

EAST INDIA

3 Oz. Brandy
½ Oz. Pineapple Juice
½ Oz. Curacao
1 Dash Bitters

Stir well with ice. Strain into sour glass.

HARRY'S PICK-ME-UP

2 Oz. Cognac
1 Teaspoon Grenadine
Juice of ½ Lemon
Champagne

Shake well with ice. Strain into Champagne glass. Fill with iced Champagne.

PRAIRIE OYSTER

1½ Oz. Brandy
1 Egg
1 Dash Worcestershire Sauce
Salt if desired

Carefully break egg into Old Fashioned glass. Add Worcestershire Sauce and Brandy. Blend lightly with egg white, keeping yolk intact.

SARATOGA

1½ Oz. Brandy
2 Dashes Pineapple Syrup
2 Dashes Maraschino
2 Dashes Bitters

Shake with cracked ice. Strain into cocktail glass. Add dash of soda.

SIDE CAR

1 Oz. Brandy
1 Oz. Triple Sec
1 Oz. Lemon Juice

Shake with cracked ice. Strain into cocktail glass.

CORDIALS & APERITIFS

ADONIS

2 Oz. Dry Sherry
1 Oz. Sweet Vermouth
1 Dash Orange Bitters

Stir well with ice. Strain into cocktail glass.

ANGEL'S TIP

1½ Oz. Creme de Cacao
½ Oz. Cream

Pour carefully into cordial glass in order given, so ingredients do not mix.

BAMBOO

1 Oz. Sherry
1 Oz. Sweet Vermouth
1 Dash Bitters

Stir well with ice. Strain into cocktail glass.

GLAD EYE

2 Oz. Anisette
1 Oz. Peppermint

Shake well with ice. Strain into cocktail glass.

GREEN ROOM

2 Oz. Dry Vermouth
1 Oz. Brandy
2 Dashes Curacao

Stir well with ice. Strain into cocktail glass.

NO. 1

2 Oz. Anisette
1 Oz. Water
1 Dash Sugar Syrup
1 Dash Bitters

Shake well with ice. Strain into cocktail glass.

PANSY

1½ Oz. Anisette
2 Dashes Grenadine
2 Dashes Bitters

Shake well with ice. Strain into cocktail glass.

PORT SANGAREE

2 Oz. Port
1 Oz. Water
½ Teaspoon Powdered
Sugar

Stir well with ice. Strain into cocktail glass. Or serve in Old Fashioned glass.

POUSSE-CAFE

¼ Oz. Grenadine
½ Oz. Creme de Cacao
½ Oz. Green Creme
de Menthe
½ Oz. Anisette
¼ Oz. Cognac or
Brandy

Pour carefully into cordial glass in order given. May be served with Brandy burning.

SANCTUARY

1 Oz. Dry Vermouth
1 Oz. Curacao
1 Oz. Triple Sec

Stir well with ice. Strain into cocktail glass.

SUISSE

1½ Oz. Anesone or
Abisante
½ Oz. Anisette
1 Egg White

Shake well with ice. Strain into cocktail glass.

UPSTAIRS

3 Oz. Sweet Vermouth
Juice of ¼ Lemon

Pour into large cocktail glass over ice cubes. Fill with soda.

WEEP NO MORE

1 Oz. Sweet Vermouth
1 Oz. Brandy
1 Oz. Lime Juice
I Dash Maraschino

Shake well with ice. Strain into cocktail glass.

OTHER DRINKS

CHAMPAGNE COCKTAIL

Champagne
1 Small Lump Sugar
1 Dash Bitters
1 Twist Lemon Peel
1 Twist Orange Peel

Place sugar in Champagne glass. Add bitters, orange and lemon peel. Fill with iced Champagne.

CHICAGO COCKTAIL

1½ Oz. Brandy
1 Dash Curacao
1 Dash Bitters
Champagne

Stir well with ice. Strain into Champagne glass frosted by wetting rim with water and dipping into sugar. Fill with iced Champagne.

JACK ROSE

1½ Oz. Applejack
½ Oz. Grenadine
Juice of ½ Lime
Shake well with ice. Strain into cocktail glass.

MERRY WIDOW

1 Oz. Cherry Brandy
1 Oz. Maraschino
Shake well with ice. Serve with cherry in a cocktail glass.

SHERRY COBBLER

Sherry
1 Teaspoon Sugar
1 Teaspoon Orange Juice
Fill highball glass ⅔ full of cracked ice. Add sugar and orange juice. Fill with Sherry. Stir slightly. Decorate with fruit and serve.

CHAPTER THREE

AROUND THE WORLD IN 31 DRINKS

PARTY PREFERENCES FROM EVERY CONTINENT

Most people have a natural urge to travel.

It answers a need for new experience and adventure.

Next time you give a party, why not create a "World Tour." It's fun. Your invitation can be in the form of a travel ticket—promising your guests "a taste of far away places." Suggest the place with your party decorations.

Once your guests are all aboard, you can easily go places by serving cocktails with the taste and sound of distant lands.

This chapter of The Calvert Party Encyclopedia gives you a guided tour of international favorites. Here is your passport to pleasure — providing a round trip for your guests with a taste for travel. Bon voyage!

(Argentina) ROSITA COCKTAIL (Serves 6)

9 Oz. Calvert Gin
3 Oz. Brandy
2 Teaspoons Grenadine
1 Teaspoon Lemon
Juice
1½ Oz. Creme de Noya
6 Maraschino Cherries
6 Pieces Lemon Peel

Pour Gin, Brandy, grenadine, lemon juice and Creme de Noya in cocktail shaker. Shake well with ice. Pour into pre-chilled cocktail glasses. Garnish each glass with maraschino cherry and twist of lemon peel.

(Bermuda) BERMUDA SWIZZLE CUP (Serves 6)

9 Oz. Light Rum
2 Whole Eggs
4 Tablespoons Sugar
3 Teaspoons Bitters

Mix eggs, sugar and bitters in tall glass. Divide among 6 highball glasses. Add one jigger of Rum to each glass. Fill with cracked ice. Stir well.

(Brazil) BATIDA (Serves 6)

9 Oz. Rum or Brandy
8 Oz. Grapefruit Juice
8 Oz. Pineapple Juice
1 Ripe Banana cut into
small pieces
1 Teaspoon Grenadine
1 Tablespoon Lemon or
Lime Juice
1 Tablespoon Honey
1 Tablespoon Fresh or
Dried Grated
Coconut
1 Teaspoon Almond
Extract
1 Cup Finely Cracked
Ice

Pour ingredients in electric blender. Mix for at least 1 minute. Strain into pre-chilled highball glasses. Decorate with maraschino cherry or fresh mint leaf.

(Bulgaria) HOT WINE AND SPICES (Serves 6)

2 Fifths Red Wine
3 Apples peeled and
sliced thin
2 Teaspoons Cinnamon
3 Cloves
¼ Cup Sugar
1 Teaspoon Lemon
Juice

Combine all ingredients in saucepan. Bring to boil and cook over low heat for 20 minutes. Strain. Return strained mixture to saucepan and reheat. Serve very hot in cup or mug.

(Cairo) S. B. HIGHBALL

1 Oz. Calvert Gin
1 Oz. Cognac
1 Oz. Lime Juice
2 Dashes Bitters

Pour into highball glass over ice. Fill with ginger ale. Add slice of lemon and orange and sprig of mint.

(Central America) NANCITO COCKTAIL
(Serves 6)

9 Oz. Nancito or Dry Vermouth
½ Teaspoon Bitters
2 Tablespoons Lemon Juice

Pre-chill highball glasses in the refrigerator for at least 1 hour. Combine the Wine with bitters and lemon juice. Stir. Fill the glasses with cracked ice. Divide the mixture evenly among the glasses. Fill with ginger ale and serve.

(Chile) CHAMPAGNE-FRUIT COCKTAIL
(Serves 6)

6 Oz. Cognac
1 Bottle Champagne, well chilled
½ Cup Chopped Fresh Pineapple
1 Orange, peeled and sliced
½ Cup Strawberries
3 Tablespoons Sugar

Chop pineapple, orange and berries very fine. Sprinkle with sugar. Pour Cognac over mixture. Chill for at least 1 hour. Divide mixture among

6 pre-chilled champagne glasses. Fill with Champagne and serve immediately.

(Copenhagen) ANGLETERRE COCKTAIL

1 Oz. Calvert Gin
1 Oz. Apricot Liqueur
1 Oz. Orange Juice
2 Dashes Anesone or Abisante

Shake with ice. Pour into cocktail glass.

(Cuba) BACARDI COCKTAIL (Serves 6)

9 Oz. Light Rum
2 Teaspoons Grenadine
Juice of Two Lemons or Limes

Pour Rum, grenadine and lemon or lime juice in a cocktail shaker with cracked ice. Shake well. Strain into pre-chilled cocktail glasses.

(England) GIN AND IT

2 Oz. Calvert Gin
1 Oz. Sweet Vermouth

Gently pour Vermouth and Calvert Gin into pitcher. Stir but do not shake. Do not add ice. Pour into cocktail glass. Serve at room temperature. Rub lemon peel on edge of glass.

(France) VERMOUTH CASSIS

1 Oz. Creme de Cassis, Black Currant or Blackberry Syrup
3 Oz. French Vermouth

Mix vermouth and Creme de Cassis. Pour into highball glass over ice cubes. Fill glass with soda and stir lightly.

(French Riviera)
MIMI COCKTAIL

1½ Oz. Calvert Gin

¾ Oz. Apricot Flavored Brandy

¾ Oz. Cognac

1 Egg White

Pour in shaker with cracked ice. Add dash of lemon juice and grenadine. Shake vigorously. Pour into cocktail glass. Prepare glass in advance by rubbing rim with lemon and powdered sugar.

(The Guianas) GEORGE-TOWN RUM SWIZZLE
(Serves 6)

9 Oz. Rum

2 Tablespoons Cherry Brandy

4 Oz. Lemon or Lime Juice

8 Oz. Cup Fresh Grapefruit Juice

2 Tablespoons Grenadine

½ Teaspoon Bitters

6 Slices Fresh Pineapple

6 Maraschino Cherries

6 Slices Orange

6 Slices Lemon

6 Springs Mint or 1 Teaspoon Liquid Mint Flavoring

2 Cups Finely Cracked Ice

Pour cracked ice, Rum, lemon or lime juice, grapefruit juice, grenadine, Cherry Brandy and bitters in pitcher. Stir until ice-cold. Arrange pineapple slice, maraschino cherry, orange slice, lemon slice and a sprig of mint in each highball glass. Fill glass about three-fourths full and add soda.

(Haiti) HAITIAN RUM PUNCH (Serves 10-12)

1 Fifth Rum

3 Teaspoons Sugar

3 Teaspoons Lemon Juice

1 Tablespoon Nutmeg

Mint Leaves

Combine sugar, lemon juice and nutmeg in mixing glass. Stir until sugar is dissolved. Add cracked ice, then Rum. Stir. Garnish with fresh mint leaves or use mint flavoring. Serve in highball glasses.

(Hong Kong)
GIMLET (Serves 6)

9 Oz. Calvert Gin

3 Tablespoons Powdered Sugar

Juice of 5 Lemons

Shake over cracked ice. Strain and pour into cocktail glasses about two-thirds full. Fill each glass with soda. Serve ice-cold.

(Indonesia) EAST INDIES COCKTAIL
(Serves 6)

   8 Oz. Brandy
   1 Tablespoon Curacao
   1 Tablespoon
      Pineapple Juice
   2 Teaspoons
      Maraschino or
      Cherry Brandy
   1 Teaspoon Bitters
   6 Slices Lemon Peel

Combine Brandy, Curacao, pineapple juice, Maraschino or Cherry Brandy and bitters in mixing glass. Add cracked ice and stir well. Pour into pre-chilled cocktail or champagne glasses. Add twist of lemon peel.

(Ireland) IRISH WHISKEY HIGHBALL

   1½ Oz. Irish Whiskey

Pour into highball glass over ice cubes. Add lemon peel. Fill glass with ginger ale.

(Jamaica) PLANTER'S PUNCH

   1½ Oz. Jamaica Rum
   1 Dash Aromatic Bitters
   Juice of ½ Lime or Lemon
   1 Teaspoon Sugar
   1 Half-Slice Orange
   1 Maraschino Cherry

Fill highball glass with finely cracked ice. Add dash of bitters, lemon juice, sugar and Rum. Stir until cold. Garnish with orange slice and cherry. Serve with straw.

(Moscow) RUSSIAN

   1½ Oz. Vodka

Pour into an Old Fashioned glass over cracked ice.

(Nicaragua) ROMPOPE
(Serves 4)

   4 Oz. Rum or Brandy
   2 Egg Yolks
   1 Quart Milk
   1 Cup Sugar
   1 Tablespoon
      Corn Meal
   ½ Stick Cinnamon or
      ½ Teaspoon Powdered Cinnamon
   1 Teaspoon Grated
      Lemon Rind
   1 Teaspoon Vanilla
      Extract

Beat egg yolks in saucepan until light. Add milk, sugar, and corn meal. Cook over low heat, stirring constantly until the mixture is syrupy. Remove from fire. Beat about 10 minutes until cool. In separate bowl combine Rum or Brandy, cinnamon, lemon rind and vanilla. Mix. Set aside both mixtures for three hours. Strain liquor mixture. Combine with milk mixture and chill. Serve ice-cold in cup or mug.

(Peru) PISCO SOUR
(Serves 6)

   9 Oz. Pisco
      (or Muscat brandy)
   1½ Oz. Sugar Syrup
   1½ Oz. Lime Juice
   ½ Teaspoon Bitters
   1 Egg White
   Cracked Ice

Stir Pisco, sugar syrup, lime juice and bitters in cocktail shaker. When well-mixed, add egg white and cracked ice. Shake well. Serve immediately in sour glass.

(The Philippines) MANILA COCKTAIL
(Serves 6)

9 Oz. Calvert Gin
4½ Oz. Sweet
  Vermouth
2 Tablespoons Cherry
  Brandy
½ Can Sweetened
  Pineapple Juice
6 Egg Whites

Boil pineapple juice in saucepan rapidly until only 2 tablespoons of syrup remain. Cool for 3 minutes. Pour pineapple juice, vermouth, egg whites, Gin and Cherry Brandy in shaker. Add ice. Shake vigorously. Pour into pre-chilled cocktail glasses. Decorate with a maraschino cherry.

(Puerto Rico) FROZEN DAIQUIRI (Serves 6)

9 Oz. Light Rum
2 Tablespoons
  Powdered Sugar
5 Tablespoons Lime
  or Lemon Juice

Pour sugar, lime or lemon juice and Rum in electric blender. Add finely cracked ice. Run blender for about 2 minutes. Pour into pre-chilled cocktail glasses and serve immediately. Small straws may be served.

(Rome) SPRUISS COCKTAIL

2 Oz. Calvert Gin
1 Oz. Apricot Flavored
  Brandy
Juice of ½ Orange
1 Dash Bitters

Shake vigorously with cracked ice. Pour into cocktail glass. Add cherry.

(Scotland) HOT PINT
(Serves 4)

4 Oz. Scotch Whiskey
32 Oz. Ale
1 Egg, beaten
4 Tablespoons Sugar

Heat ale to the boiling point. Combine egg, sugar and Scotch. Mix well. Gradually add boiling ale, stirring constantly to prevent curdling. Pour into mugs from a height, to create froth. Drink immediately with froth.

(Singapore) SINGAPORE GIN SLING (Serves 6)

- 9 Oz. Calvert Gin
- 1½ Oz. Cherry Brandy
- 2 Tablespoons Powdered Sugar
- Juice of 2 Lemons
- 6 Maraschino Cherries
- 6 Finger-length Slices Fresh Pineapple

Mix powdered sugar, Gin, Cherry Brandy and lemon juice in cocktail shaker. Half-fill highball glases with cracked ice. Place a cherry and a piece of pineapple in each glass. Add the liquor and fill each glass with carbonated water. Serve ice-cold. Add a fresh strawberry or paper-thin slices of lemon or orange, if available.

(Stockholm) WHITE LADY COCKTAIL

- 1 Oz. Calvert Gin
- 1 Oz. Triple Sec
- 1 Oz. Lemon Juice
- 1 Teaspoon Powdered Sugar

Shake well with crushed ice. Strain. Serve in cocktail glass with cherry.

(Sweden) TRADITIONAL SWEDISH CHRISTMAS GLUG (Serves 6)

- 16 Oz. Brandy
- 16 Oz. Red Wine (Burgundy or Claret)
- 16 Oz. Port Wine
- 1 Tablespoon finely chopped Orange or Lemon Peel
- ¼ Pound Cube Sugar
- ¼ Pound Seedless Raisins
- 5 Cardamon Seeds
- 1 Cinnamon Stick (or 2 teaspoons powdered cinnamon)
- 5 Cloves
- ¼ Pound Blanched Almonds

Combine the Red Wine and Port in saucepan over low heat. Place orange peel, cardamon seeds, cinnamon and cloves in cheescloth. Tie or sew cheesecloth securely. Place in Wine mixture. Simmer for 20 minutes. Then remove.

Place cubes of sugar in metal strainer. Rest on top of the saucepan. Set Brandy aflame and pour slowly over sugar. As lighted Brandy is poured over sugar, it will caramelize. (As an alternative, ½ cup of granulated sugar may be dissolved in Wine. Brandy is set aflame and poured into Wine.) Serve in heated mugs.

(Tokyo) MOUNT FUJI
(Individual Serving)

1½ Oz. Calvert Gin
2 Teaspoons Pineapple
    Juice
3 Teaspoons Lemon
    Juice
2 Teaspoons Cream
1½ Teaspoons Sugar
    Syrup
1 Egg White
1 Dash Cherry Brandy

Shake well with cracked ice.
Pour in highball glass. Add
cherry when serving.

(Trinidad) TRINIDAD RUM PUNCH (Serves 6)

9 Oz. Rum
3 Oz. Water
3 Oz. Sugar
1 Cup Cracked Ice
⅛ Teaspoon Bitters
3 Oz. Lime or Lemon
    Juice
6 Pieces Lime or Lemon
    Rind

Combine water and sugar in
a saucepan. Bring to boil
and cook over low heat for
15 minutes. Cool for 1 hour.
Place cracked ice in pitcher.
Add bitters, lime or lemon
juice, Rum, and sugar syrup.
Mix well. Pour in highball
glasses, decorate with lime
or lemon rind.

(Yugoslavia) WINE LIQUEUR (Serves 8)

16 Oz. Brandy
1 Quart Red Wine
1¼ Cups Sugar
2 Teaspoons Vanilla
    Extract

Combine Wine and sugar in
a saucepan. Bring to boil
and cook over medium heat
for ten minutes. Cool for 1
hour. Add vanilla and Brandy.
Chill and serve cold. Prefer-
ably in mugs.

CHAPTER FOUR

ADD PUNCH TO THE PARTY!

14 EASY-TO-MAKE BEVERAGES FOR THE CROWD

Punch is perfect for serving large groups. Once your punch bowl is filled — guests can help themselves. Your mixing chores end right at the start.

Except for soda used in some punch recipes, your mixture may be prepared well in advance of the party. You'll improve the punch flavor by chilling it several hours before serving.

In addition to providing very pleasing refreshment — your punch bowl can perform as a striking centerpiece. It's simple. Here's how: prior to the party — take a large block of ice. Fill your punch bowl with hot water. Place it on the ice block. The heat will melt out a hollow mold. When the mold is deep enough, remove the hot water. Then set your punch bowl in the fresh ice hollow. It will keep your punch chilled right down to the last serving — and provide a novel conversation piece. Be sure your punch bowl is made of metal or a non breakable material.

Here is a tempting variety of punch recipes. Each one is sure to leave every guest pleased as punch.

WHISKEY PUNCHES

ARTILLERY PUNCH
(25 to 30 cups)

1 Quart Calvert Extra
½ Pint Calvert Gin
½ Pint Brandy
1½ Oz. Claristine or
  Benedictine
1 Bottle Red Wine
1 Pint Dark Rum
1 Quart Strong Tea
1 Pint Orange Juice
½ Pint Lemon Juice

Combine ingredients in large punch bowl. Add block of ice. Sugar syrup may be added for sweetening. Decorate with twists of lemon peel. Serve in punch cups.

MILK PUNCH (Basic)
(Serves 14)

1 Quart Calvert Extra
3 Quarts Milk
4 Oz. Powdered Sugar

Place in punch bowl over ice cubes. Beat well. Strain into mug or glass. Sprinkle with nutmeg.

WHISKEY PUNCH
(Serves 13)

1 Quart Calvert Extra
1½ Oz. Curacao
Juice of 3 Lemons
Juice of 4 Oranges
1 Tablespoon Sugar

Mix ingredients. Pour over block of ice in punch bowl. Add fruits as desired plus 1 quart chilled soda or iced tea. Serve in punch cups.

This is probably the most famous and widely used punch recipe.

SCOTCH WHISKY PUNCH (Serves 12)

1 Quart Scotch
Juice and Rind of
  3 Lemons
½ Cup Sugar
1 Quart Soda

Combine in pitcher with cracked ice. Pour into goblets with extra ice. Garnish with fruit slices.

GIN PUNCHES

BACCIO (Serves 8)

8 Oz. Calvert Gin
3 Oz. Anisette
8 Oz. Grapefruit Juice
Champagne

Combine in punch bowl over block of ice. Add sugar syrup to taste, orange slices, lemon slices. Before serving add 1 split chilled Champagne and 16 oz. chilled soda. Serve in punch cups.

GIN PUNCH NO. 1
(Serves 8)

1 Quart Calvert Gin
1 Oz. Sugar
8 Twists Lemon Peel
Juice of 4 Lemons
½ Oz. Maraschino
1 Quart Soda

Mix in punch bowl. Add ice, chilled soda. Stir. Serve in punch cups.

GIN PUNCH NO. 2
(Serves 20-24)

2 Quarts Calvert Gin
Juice of 12 Lemons
Juice of 20 Oranges
6 Oz. Grenadine
2 Quarts Soda

Combine and pour over large block of ice. Add chilled soda. Decorate with fruit. Serve in punch cups.

GIN SWIZZLE
(Serves 10)

1 Pint Calvert Gin
2 Oz. Sugar Syrup
4 Oz. Lime Juice
10 Dashes Bitters

Stir until foamy. Add ice. Pour into cocktail glasses.

PINEAPPLE PUNCH
(Serves 10)

4 Oz. Calvert Gin
1½ Quarts Moselle
 Wine
Juice of 3 Lemons

5 Dashes Bitters
1 Oz. Pineapple Syrup
1 Oz. Grenadine
1 Oz. Maraschino
1 Quart Soda

Combine in punch bowl with 1 quart chilled soda. Set bowl in bed of crushed ice. Decorate with pineapple. Serve in punch cups.

RUM PUNCHES

BRIDE'S BOWL
(Serves 20)

1½ Quarts Light Rum
½ Pineapple, sliced
1 Pint Strawberries
¾ Cup Sugar Syrup
1 Cup Lemon Juice
2 Cups Pineapple Juice

Chill for 2 hours. Serve in punch bowl with block of ice, adding 1 pint thinly sliced strawberries and 2 quarts soda. Serve in punch cups.

FISH HOUSE PUNCH
(Serves 20-25)

2 Quarts Light Rum
1 Quart Cognac
4 Oz. Peach Brandy
¾ Pound Sugar (or ½
 Pint Sugar Syrup)
1½ Pints Lemon Juice
3½ Pints Water

Dissolve sugar in part of the water in punch bowl. Add

the lemon juice and balance of water. Stir thoroughly. Add the liquor. Allow mixture to stand for 2 to 3 hours, stirring from time to time. Place large block of ice in a bowl, stir to cool, and serve. Serve in punch cups.

STIRRUP CUP (Serves 8)

1 Pint Light Rum
1½ Oz. Brown Sugar,
   dissolved in water
3 Oz. Lime Juice
6 Oz. Pineapple Juice

Serve in punch bowl with ice. Provide highball glasses filled with cracked ice and decorated with lemon peel spiral.

VODKA PUNCHES

VODKA BOMBAY PUNCH (Serves 12)

1 Quart Vodka
1 Quart Sherry
¼ Pint Maraschino
½ Pint Curacao
2 Quarts Chilled Soda

Combine in a mixing bowl, without ice. Set punch bowl in bed of crushed ice. Decorate with fruits. Add 4 quarts chilled Champagne just before serving. Serve in punch cups.

HOT-BLOODED MARY (Serves 15)

1 Quart Vodka
1 Large Can Tomato
   Juice (1 Qt., 14 Oz.)
2-Inch Stick of
   Cinnamon
⅛ Teaspoon Cloves
1 Tablespoon Worces-
   tershire Sauce

Combine tomato juice, cinnamon, cloves, Worcestershire Sauce. Cook over low heat about 15 minutes. Add salt and pepper to taste. Add lemon juice just before serving. Pour in Vodka. Use Old Fashioned glasses or demi-tasse cups.

CHAPTER FIVE

EASY TO MAKE TINY TEMPTERS

42 HORS D'OEUVRES, DIPS AND CANAPES TO SPREAD YOUR REPUTATION AS A KNOWING HOST OR HOSTESS

Good food goes hand-in-hand with good drink and good company. Colorful and tempting snacks give any party a big lift. This chapter of The Calvert Party Encyclopedia is designed to give every hostess a wide choice of mouth-watering tid-bits.

Your spread of tempting canapes can be prepared ahead of time. Keeping them fresh is easy. Just cover your trays with wax paper and a damp kitchen towel. Store them in your refrigerator until time to serve. Don't store toasted or cracker-based canapes this way, however.

Hot hors d'oeuvres can be kept ready in a warm oven. Chafing dishes or electrically heated trays are ideal, too.

Party after party — bite for bite — each of the following treats is sure to win lip-smacking approval.

SARDINE DIP

Blend ½ lb. cream cheese with 3 tbs. lime juice. Add 2 tins of sardines mashed with their own oil, 3 tbs. finely cut chives and ½ cup chopped parsley. Add salt to taste. Then cream to dipping consistency.

CALVERT BLEU CHEESE SPREAD

Place ½ lb. Bleu Cheese in small mixing bowl. Cover with Calvert Extra. Marinate in refrigerator for 2 hours. Blend Cheese thoroughly with 4 tbs. cream cheese. Add 2 stalks finely chopped celery and blend again. Wrap securely and chill in refrigerator overnight. To serve, place in wooden bowl surrounded by salted crackers.

HAM BALLS

Combine 6 chopped, hard-cooked eggs, 1 tbs. minced chives or onions, ½ cup ground cooked ham, ground pepper, ¼ cup mayonnaise. Shape into small balls. Roll balls in ⅔ cup of chopped walnuts.

LOBSTER Á LA CALVERT

Mix 2 cups cooked rock lobster tails, cut into small pieces, with ½ cup mayonnaise. Add 1 tbs. tomato ketchup, 2 tsp. lemon juice, 2 tsp. finely chopped parsley, 2 tsp. finely chopped chives (or onions), salt, pepper to taste, and 2 tbs. Calvert Extra. Serve with cocktail picks or melba rounds.

SHRIMP REMOULADE

In a bowl, place 1 cup mayonnaise with 1 tsp. prepared mustard and 1 tsp. each of minced gherkins, capers, parsley, chives. Add ½ minced clove of garlic and ½ tsp. anchovy paste. Salt and pepper to taste. Mix thoroughly. This is sufficient sauce for 2 lbs. of cooked shrimp. Store in refrigerator. Serve sauce, thoroughly chilled, in bowl surrounded by ice-cold shrimp, each jabbed with toothpick.

WATER CRESS CORNUCOPIAS

Twist paper-thin slices of Italian salami into cornucopia shapes, rolled together at base and open at top. Fill with sprigs of crisp water cress, so that the leaves emerge from top. Secure with picks.

CHEESE WHEELS

Mix 1½ lb. dry cottage cheese, 1 beaten egg, 4 tbs. caraway seed, 1 tbs. sugar and 4 tbs. melted butter. Blend thoroughly and form into small balls. Bake cheese balls in moderate oven (350°) for about 15 minutes. Chill. Serve ice-cold, jabbing each cheese morsel with a pretzel stick.

SMOKED TURKEY "CIGARETTES"

On paper-thin slices of smoked turkey, spread seasoned cream cheese and roll into "cigarettes." Pierce with cocktail picks.

AVOCADO HAM SPREAD

Mash half-ripe avocado with canned deviled-ham spread. Serve with corn chips.

FRENCH-DRESSED MUSHROOMS

Drain juice from canned mushrooms. Add French dressing to mushrooms. Chill well. Drain, serve on toothpicks.

CHEESE LOGS

1 cup pecans
1 clove garlic
1 six-oz. pkg. cream cheese
1 tbs. A-1 Sauce
1½ tsb. chili powder

Finely grind pecans and garlic clove. Blend together with cream cheese and A-1 Sauce. Shape into roll about 5 inches long and 1½ inches in diameter. Roll in chili powder to coat evenly. Wrap in foil and chill until firm. Slice and serve with crisp crackers.

PICKLE ROLL-UPS

Remove crust from sliced bread and spread slices with cream cheese. Roll each slice of bread tightly around large sweet cucumber pickle. Chill thoroughly and slice to serve.

STUFFED CELERY

Wash and dry celery. Cut into 1½ inch lengths. Fill hollows with:

A. Cream cheese, strongly seasoned with Worcestershire Sauce, tomato ketchup and French dressing.

B. Cream cheese and Roquefort cheese, blended with mayonnaise, lemon juice and salt and pepper.

C. Caviar, sprinkled with a few drops of lemon juice. Any prepared cheese spread. Garnish tray with parsley.

POLKA DOT

Combine mashed anchovies, mashed hard-boiled egg yolks and Parmesan cheese. Add cream to moisten and a dash of cayenne. Spread on crackers.

HAM 'N' EGGS

Cut hard-boiled eggs lengthwise in half and remove yolks. Fill whites with finely ground ham, liberally mixed with mayonnaise. Arrange on a platter and serve with crackers. (Blend yolks with mayonnaise, pepper to taste, and spread on crackers.)

HOT HOUSE

Mix Limburger cheese with small amount of butter. Add grated onion and sprinkle liberally with salt. Spread on crackers.

TONGUE TREAT

Combine ground cooked tongue, cooked mushrooms, a chopped dill pickle with a liberal helping of Thousand Island Dressing. Spread on unsalted crackers.

PICKLE CANAPES

A very decorative canape.

Remove the crust from slices of fresh white bread, using sharp thin-bladed knife.

Mash Roquefort or soft cream cheese thinned with cream. Color mixture pink with paprika.

Spread on bread slices. Roll each slice around jumbo pickle. Wrap rolls in waxed paper. Chill. When ready to serve cut into ¼ inch slices.

FILLED EDAM CHEESE

Hollow Edam or Gouda cheese. Crumble removed part. Combine with:

2 teaspoons or more Worcestershire Sauce to taste
1 tablespoon prepared mustard
a few grains of cayenne
1 or 2 tablespoons fresh or dried herbs, minced

Refill cheese shell. Serve surrounded by toasted crackers.

LOBSTER BITES

Mix finely chopped lobster meat with lemon juice, pepper, salt, mayonnaise and a small amount of French dressing. Serve on toast squares.

DIPPER'S DELIGHT

Cream equal portions of Roquefort and cream cheese. Add sour cream to smooth. Serve in a shallow dish as potato chip dip.

CHIVE BALLS

Mix equal parts of grated Swiss cheese and minced ham. Add one egg yolk, mustard and salt. Roll in minced chives. Form into small balls and serve with party picks.

ROYAL RELISH

Prepare a mixture of cream cheese and India relish. Spread on slices of dried beef. Roll. Fasten with party picks and chill before serving.

TINY 'BURGERS

Combine 2 lbs. of finely ground beef, ½ cup bread crumbs, 2 tbs. minced onions, parsley, one raw egg. Season to taste. Shape into tiny meat balls. Into saucepan pour contents of 8 oz. can of tomato spaghetti sauce. Place 'burgers in sauce and simmer about 10 minutes. Store in refrigerator. To serve, just heat in chafing dish at buffet table. Supply cocktail picks.

CHEESE BREEZE

Mix cheddar cheese with several strips of broiled bacon. Spread on toast triangles and place in broiler until brown. Serve piping hot.

SALAMI SAVORIES

Mix can condensed celery soup with cream cheese until creamy. Add finely ground salami. Spread on toast squares. Heat in broiler until browned.

HOT RIPE OLIVES

Drain can of ripe olives. Add 1 clove of minced garlic to the liquid. Boil liquid. Add olives. Drain as soon as they are hot. Serve hot olives on toothpicks.

TIDBITS IN BLANKETS

Select any of these tidbits. Wrap in thin strip of bacon. Secure with toothpicks. Broil under moderate heat until bacon is crisp.

Cooked Shrimp
Oysters
Stuffed olives
Pickled onions
Watermelon pickle
Sautéed chicken livers

CHICKEN LIVER AND BACON HORS D'OEUVRES

Cook chicken livers in boiling salted water for 20 minutes, or until tender. Drain. Wrap each cooked chicken liver in ½ slice of bacon, cut crosswise. Fasten bacon in place with wooden toothpicks. Broil or bake until delicately browned, turning occasionally. Serve hot with toothpicks still in place.

SAVORIES

Put the following items through food chopper:

½ pound cheddar cheese
8 slices crisp bacon
2 small onions
Blend with 1 teaspoon dry mustard
2 teaspoons mayonnaise

Spread on slices of bread. Toast under broiler until golden brown. Cut into triangles and serve hot.

CHAPTER SIX

PARTY PERFECT FOODS

15 SUMPTUOUS RECIPES SIMPLE TO PREPARE, SPECTACULAR TO EAT

THE LAST WORD IN GOOD TASTE

Many parties will feature food as a main attraction. The drinks and tidbits are only curtain-raisers.

On these occasions, you'll want your main dish to excel — to win the praise of hearty appetites.

Here is an appealing and delicious lineup of chef's delights. Yet — you can prepare them easily and economically. Serve buffet style — and watch the first taste start the stampede for seconds!

CHILI CON CARNE (MILD) (serves 8)

Melt 2 tablespoons bacon drippings or butter
Saute in the fat ½ cup chopped onion or ½ clove minced garlic
Add 1 pound ground beef
Stir and saute until well-done. Add contents of:
1 (10½ oz.) can condensed tomato soup
1 No. 2 can kidney beans
2 tablespoons chili powder
¾ teaspoon or more of salt to taste
Cover and cook slowly for 1 hour

CHOW MEIN WITH FRIED NOODLES (serves 10)

(May be prepared in advance and reheated.)
Cut ½ lb. lean pork into cubes.
Melt 3 tablespoons butter in skillet.
Add 2 tablespoons minced onions and cook for 2 minutes.
Brown meat in butter. Stir in 2½ tablespoons flour.
When flour is blended, stir in slowly 2½ cups chicken stock.

Add:
¼ teaspoon salt
¼ teaspoon paprika
1½ cups diced cooked chicken
¾ cup diced celery or bean sprouts
¾ cup mushrooms, canned or fresh
Simmer these ingredients gently for ½ hour. or cook in double boiler.

Add 2 tablespoons soy sauce (optional) and additional seasoning, if needed. Serve chow mein on large deep platter. Surround with fried noodles.

BAKED CHICKEN MOUSSE (serves 10)

1 cup rich Cream Sauce*
Cook slightly and add: 2 egg yolks
Combine sauce with:
2 cups cooked ground chicken
½ cup dry bread crumbs
½ teaspoon salt
½ teaspoon pepper
1 tablespoon chopped parsley
Whip until stiff and fold in 2 egg whites.

Pour ingredients into mold lined with waxed paper. Set in a pan of hot water and bake mousse in moderate 325° oven for 1 hour.
Serve with canned mushroom sauce.

*(See Recipe For Cream Sauce on Page 73)

BEEF STROGANOFF (serves 4)

Cut 1½ pounds fillet of beef into ½ inch slices.
Pound beef with a mallet until thin. Cut into strips about 1 inch wide. Melt 1 tablespoon butter in pan.

Saute ¾ tablespoon minced onion in butter for 2 minutes.

Saute beef quickly in butter for about 5 minutes. Turn evenly. Remove beef. Keep it hot. Add 2 tablespoons butter to the pan. Slice ¾ pound mushrooms and add, stir and saute in the butter. Add the beef. Season with:

Salt
Paprika
A grating of nutmeg
½ teaspoon basil (optional)
Add ½ cup warm sour cream and heat, but do not boil.

SALMON AND RICE DELIGHT (serves 4)

Line casserole with cooked rice. Flake two 7-oz. cans of salmon finely on top of rice. Pour salmon liquid over fish. Cover with more rice. Pour in:
1 egg, well beaten
¼ cup milk
Season with salt and pepper
Dot with butter. Bake in 375° oven for 30 minutes.

TURKEY TETRAZZINI (serves 8)

Cook until brown and crisp:
  2 slices bacon, finely cut
Add and brown lightly in the bacon fat:
  ⅓ cup minced onion
  ½ cup minced green pepper
Add: 2 cups grated American cheese (½ lb.)
  ¼ cup cut-up pimiento
  ¼ cup toasted shaved almonds
  1¾ cups cooked peas
  2 cups cut-up turkey or chicken (cooked)

Mix lightly with hot drained boiled macaroni (8 oz. un-cooked). Heat, using turkey or chicken stock (or con-somme) to moisten. Serve hot with tomato slices, parsley, and ripe olives.

JAMBALAYA (serves 6)

2 chopped onions	2 minced garlic buds
1 tbs. butter	3 fresh tomatoes
1 tbs. flour	2 cans crab meat or shrimp
1 bay leaf	½ cup diced ham
1 pinch thyme	3 cups cooked rice
1 pinch parsley	

Saute onions in butter. Add flour and blend. Season with bay leaf, thyme, parsley and minced garlic buds. Cook 5 minutes. Add tomatoes. Simmer 10 minutes. Add crab meat or shrimp. Simmer 5 minutes. Add diced ham and cooked rice. Serve at once.

VEAL SCALOPPINE (serves 4)

1 lb. leg of veal, sliced ⅛-inch thick	1 cup Sauterne wine
	2 teaspoons lemon juice
⅛ lb. butter	Flour, seasoned with salt, pepper
Pinch of thyme	

Cut meat into serving-size pieces and roll in seasoned flour. Heat butter in heavy frying pan and brown floured meat. Lower flame, add wine, lemon juice and thyme. Cover and let simmer about 30 minutes, or until meat is very tender.

INDIA CHICKEN CURRY
(serves 10-12)

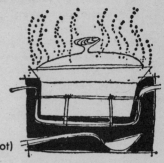

½ cup finely chopped onions
½ cup finely chopped celery
4 tablespoons butter or chicken fat
⅓ cup flour
2 cups chicken stock
1 cup strained tomato juice
½ teaspoon Worcestershire Sauce
1 teaspoon curry powder
Salt and pepper to taste
4 cups cooked diced chicken or turkey (hot)
4 cups hot, steamed rice

Simmer onions and celery in butter until yellow. Add flour and mix thoroughly. Add stock and cook until smooth and thick. Add tomato juice and seasonings, then chicken. Heat thoroughly. Pack rice into greased ring mold and let stand in warm place 10 minutes. Unmold and fill center with hot, curried chicken.

FROZEN FRUIT SALAD
(serves 10-12)

3 3-oz. packages cream cheese
1 cup mayonnaise
1 pint whipping cream
1 cup diced bananas or seeded
   white grapes
1 cup crushed pineapple
1 cup pitted cherries

Blend cheese and mayonnaise. Fold in whipped cream and add fruits. Pour into refrigerator tray and freeze. Serve on crisp lettuce.

ASPARAGUS LOAF (serves 8)

1 No. 2 can green asparagus tips
1 pimiento, cut in strips
5 egg yolks
2 tablespoons flour
1 tablespoon butter
1¾ cups milk
1 teaspoon salt
¼ teaspoon pepper
5 stiff-beaten egg whites

Line greased shallow loaf pan with asparagus tips. Garnish with pimiento strip. Beat egg yolks until thick and lemon-colored. Add white sauce made of flour, butter, milk and seasonings. Fold in egg whites. Pour over asparagus. Place pan in hot water. Bake in moderate oven (350 degrees) 45-50 minutes or until set. Unmold on platter and pour ¼ cup melted butter over top.

BUNCH OF GRAPES (serves 6)

6 pear halves
2 3-oz. packages cream cheese
½ pound Tokay grapes

Drain pears, turn cut side down, and spread with softened cheese. Halve grapes, remove seeds, and press into the cheese, placing close together. Serve on lettuce leaf with dressing.

MUSHROOMS AU GRATIN (serves 6)

Cook small can mushrooms and add to cream sauce.*

Place in greased baking dish. Cover top with butter. Sprinkle with grated cheddar cheese. Heat over a moderate flame.

*(See Recipe For Cream Sauce on Next Page)

MULLED CUCUMBERS

(serves 6)

Pare, seed and cut cucumbers into strips. (Enough for 1½ cupsful)
Drop into 1½ cups boiling water
Add ½ teaspoon salt
Cook until nearly tender. Drain well. Place ¾ cup Cream Sauce in
　double boiler
Season sauce with:
Salt
Paprika
A few grains of nutmeg (optional)

If sauce is made with sweet milk or cream, add 1 teaspoon
or more lemon juice.

When sauce is boiling, add drained cucumbers. Place over
hot water and steam for several minutes before serving.

CREAM SAUCE

Melt 1 tablespoon butter in saucepan. Slowly add 3 tablespoons sifted flour. Add 1 cup of milk, more or less, to
desired consistency.

CHAPTER SEVEN

36
UNUSUAL
NIGHTS

Exciting Ideas to Make Your Party an Event!

"Something new and different . . . out of the ordinary." This is what people like most about going to a party. And with a little imagination you can make your party an event. All it takes is a theme or an idea. Once you decide on a novel twist — let your guests know in advance. They'll look forward to a unique evening — and will come prepared to help with the fun.

Here are a number of suggestions. They will start you on your way to new and exciting parties your guests will long remember.

Four Planned Parties

1. Monte Carlo Party

This event has built-in games, entertainment and decor. Buy, rent or borrow a roulette wheel, dice, playing cards. From neighbors and friends, obtain extra card tables. Cover tables with green tablecloths or green felt. Set one gambling game up at each table. As each guest arrives, present him or her with a supply of chips or play money. Your guests will spend most of the evening entertaining themselves.

Give your cocktails names such as: "Gambler's Demise," or "Daredevil Punch," or "All or Nothing," etc. At an appointed time, e.g., Midnight, stop all gambling and award a prize to the guest who has won the most chips. Dice motifs will add to your decor. "Good Luck" canapes are in order, or use standard canapes with "Bona Fortuna" names.

2. Pirate Party

Your swashbuckling friends will excel at this party. Perfect as a masquerade party. Decor should involve treasure, "jolly rogers," anything out of "Treasure Island." Food should have a Caribbean flair. (See Jambalaya — page 70)

Canapes can be named "Long John Silver," "Buccaneer Bits," "Bluebeard's Blanket," etc. Drinks are "Pirate's Prize (page 39), "Walking The Plank," "Kidnapped Princess," etc.

3. Western Party

Early San Francisco or the Wild West sets the theme for this party. Costumes, if any, can be kept simple . . . cowboy hats, bandannas, etc. For a clever twist paint names on glasses with nail polish, e.g., "Sawdust Spike," "Lady Lou," "Snakeface Sam."

Each guest selects glass with Western name and uses this "new name" for the entire party. Use spurs, Cowboy and Indian themes for decor. Food should be of the "Chuck Wagon" variety, served on tin pie plates. Drinks can be named "Desert Delight," "High Noon," "Last Roundup," "Sutter's Gold," etc. Games can be quizzes on famous cowboys, or better still, Square Dance Contests.

4. Gay Nineties Party

Happy, nostalgic, light-hearted flavor is in order for Gay Nineties parties. Cardboard mustaches or derby hats for the gentlemen add a comic note . . . fans for the ladies. Decor should be Victorian.

Plan a "Barbershop Quartet" contest or a group sing. Use songs and music such as "Daisy, Daisy," "East-Side, West-Side," "Take Me Out To The Ball Game," "My Wild Irish Rose," etc. Plan some quizzes about the turn-of-the-century days. Drinks can be named after famous personalities, e.g., "Lillian Russell Cocktail," "Diamond Jim's Joy," "The Great John L.," etc. Serve pretzels, potato chips, fancy-type canapes.

CALENDAR PARTY IDEAS

PARTY	THEME	DECOR	SUGGESTED DRINK NAMES	SUGGESTED FOODS	GAMES
January Old Year Headlines	Recent News Events	Old Newspapers	"Moon Shot"	New food recipes	Current events quiz
Resolution Party	New Year's Resolutions	Proverbs	"New Leaf," "Fresh Page"	Puritan foods	Guess each others' resolutions
February St. Valentine	Hearts & Flowers	Hearts & Flowers	"Romeo & Juliet"	Heartbreak Salad	Famous lover quizzes
Washington's, Lincoln's Birthdays	Presidents	Cherries, hatchets, log cabin, etc.	"Honest George" "Old Abe"	Cherry pie	Presidents quiz
Mardi Gras	Shrove Tuesday	Fanciful, lavish	"High Jinks"	Jambalaya	Dance Contests
March St. Patrick's Day	Green	Shamrocks	"Blarney Stone"	Mulligan Stew or Irish dishes	Snake Dances Irish Jigs
April April Foolish Party	Shennanigans	Dunce caps	"Foolish Heart"	Vegetarian dishes that look like meat	Stunts
May May Day Decoration Day	Spring Patriotic	Bright flowers Flags	"Green Thumb" "Patrick Henry," "Nathan Hale"	Spring salads Ice Cream	Treasure Hunt War quizzes
June Bride & Groom	Marriage	White, wedding type	"Bride's Delight"	Wedding Cake	Romantic quizzes

PARTY	THEME	DECOR	SUGGESTED DRINK NAMES	SUGGESTED FOODS	GAMES
July Fourth of July	Fireworks	Flags, bunting	"Independence" "Firecracker"	Hot dogs	American History
August Barbecues, picnics	Summertime	Outdoors	"Heat Wave"	Hamburgers, Cool Salads	3-Legged Race Sack Race
September Labor Day	Occupations	Outdoors	"Help Wanted"	Chicken, cold	"What's My Occu- pation" quizzes
October Columbus Day Halloween	New World Witches, Ghosts	Ships Broomsticks, pumpkins	"Discovery" "Hob Goblin"	Apple pie Ghoul's canapes	Discoverer quizzes Ghost games
November Armistice Day Thanksgiving	White Flag Turkey	Army, Navy Traditional	"Victory" "Thanksgiving Cup"	V-cut canapes Turkey	War Event quizzes Apple bobbing
December Christmas	Christmas	Holly, Greens, Santa Claus	"Christmas Punch" "Eggnog"	Ham	Song Fest
New Year's Eve	New Year's Eve	Balloons, horns	"Champagne Punch"	Sandwiches	Balloon Breaking Games

BIRTHDAYS

Anybody's birthday is always a wonderful reason to give a party. Here are familiar birthstones and flowers with their sentimental "meaning." They should help spark birthday party ideas.

MONTH	BIRTHSTONE (meaning)	FLOWER (meaning)	ZODIAC SIGN
JANUARY	Garnet *Constancy*	Carnation *Friendship*	Aquarius *Water Bearer* (Jan. 20th to Feb. 18th)
FEBRUARY	Amethyst *Sincerity*	Violet-Primrose *Modesty*	Pisces *Fish* (Feb. 19th to Mar. 20th)
MARCH	Aquamarine *Courage*	Jonquil-Daffodil *Breath of Spring*	Aries *Ram* (Mar. 21st to Apr. 20th)
APRIL	Diamond *Innocence*	Daisy-Sweet Pea *Love*	Taurus *Bull* (April 21st to May 20th)
MAY	Emerald *Happiness*	Lilly of Valley-Hawthorne *Confession of Love*	Gemini *Twins* (May 21st to June 21st)
JUNE	Pearl-Moonstone *Purity*	Rose-Honeysuckle *Love, Devotion*	Cancer *Crab* (June 22nd to July 22nd)

MONTH	BIRTHSTONE (meaning)	FLOWER (meaning)	ZODIAC SIGN
JULY	Ruby *Friendship*	Water Lily-Larkspur *Ardent Attachment*	Leo *Lion* (July 23rd to Aug. 22nd)
AUGUST	Sardonyx-Peridot *Felicity*	Poppy-Gladiolus *Beauty in Retirement*	Virgo *Virgin* (Aug. 23rd to Sept. 22nd)
SEPTEMBER	Sapphire *Wisdom*	Morning Glory-Aster *Promise of Happiness*	Libra *Balance* (Sept. 23rd to Oct. 22nd)
OCTOBER	Opal-Tourmaline *Hope*	Calendula *Constancy*	Scorpio *Scorpion* (Oct. 23rd to Nov. 21st)
NOVEMBER	Topaz *Fidelity*	Chrysanthemum *Loveliness Cheerfulness*	Sagittarius *Archer* (Nov. 22nd to Dec. 21st)
DECEMBER	Turquoise *Success*	Holly-Narcissus *Precious Moments*	Capricorn *Goat* (Dec. 22nd to Jan. 19th)

ANNIVERSARIES

An anniversary is a perfect occasion for a party. Here is a list of anniversaries with their generally accepted symbols to help spark interesting party ideas.

ANNIVERSARY	ITEM
First	Paper
Second	Cotton
Third	Leather
Fourth	Flowers
Fifth	Wood
Sixth	Iron
Seventh	Wool
Eighth	Bronze
Ninth	Pottery
Tenth	Aluminum
Eleventh	Steel
Twelfth	Linen
Thirteenth	Lace
Fourteenth	Ivory
Fifteenth	Crystal
Twentieth	China
Twenty-Fifth	Silver
Thirtieth	Pearl
Thirty-Fifth	Jade
Fortieth	Ruby
Forty-Fifth	Sapphire
Fiftieth	Gold
Seventy-Fifth	Diamond

CHAPTER EIGHT

FUN AND GAMES
...ANY NUMBER CAN PLAY!

11 GAY, AMUSING PARTY IDEAS

Games are good party mixers. They get everyone to take an active part in the fun. Familiar games are usually the best ice-breakers.

Here's a handy and useful selection of games to keep your party moving right along. They require little or no preparation — and are sure-fire fun-raisers.

JUMBLED WORDS

Scramble the letters of popular movie titles, names of famous persons or titles of famous books. Give each guest a copy, along with a pencil. The one who unscrambles the complete list first, wins. Set a time limit.

Here are a few suggestions:

EREGOG SNIHANGWOT
(George Washington)
NEOG HIWT HET DNIW
(Gone With The Wind)
OWSN ITHEW DAN ETH VNEES RAWFSD
(Snow White and The Seven Dwarfs)

Slogan Guessing

Prepare a list of 20 or 30 well-known advertising slogans. Give each guest a copy; guests must identify the product associated with each slogan. The first person to identify all products correctly wins.

Some suggested samples:

Breakfast of Champions (Wheaties)
From Contented Cows (Carnation Milk)
The Soft Whiskey (Calvert Extra)
You Can Be Sure If It's (Westinghouse)
Look Sharp, Feel Sharp, Be Sharp (Gillette Blue Blades)
Progress Is Our Most Important Product (GE)
When It Rains It Pours (Morton's Salt)
His Master's Voice (RCA Victor)

Newspaper Maxims

Divide guests into teams. Teams should write out selected maxims. Give each team a strip of Scotch tape and some old magazines or newspapers. At the signal to begin, all players search the printed pages for words that fit into a familiar saying they have chosen. The shorter the maxim, the better. As they find the words, their captain pastes them on the strip of tape. First team that completes maxim, wins.

Eye Spy

Divide guests into teams of ten or less, each with a captain. Give each captain a pad of paper with the numbers one to twenty-five. Take one team at a time and have them stand around a covered card table. At a signal, remove the cover, revealing a miscellaneous selection of twenty-five articles. Allow each team one minute to view objects. Then re-cover table. The team then retires to a corner while the next team has its chance. Captains then write down all objects the members of their teams remember. The team with the longest correct list wins.

Talkathon

Provide plenty of towels and have an ice bucket full of ice cubes on hand. Choose two guests. Hand guest "A" an ice cube to hold in his right hand. Tell guest "B" to start talking and not to stop. If he stops, guest "A" hands him the cube, and "A" must start talking. Limit talks to specific topics . . . sports, politics, etc. If the guest with the ice cube cannot hold it in his right hand any longer, he may hand it to his opponent. However, he must take over the talking. When the cube has melted away, another couple starts a new Talkathon.

Charades

Guests are divided into two teams. Captain of each team receives a slip of paper on which is written a well-known adage. He reads the slip to himself and tries to convey it to his teammates in pantomine. No words may be spoken, no questions asked. As soon as his team has guessed the adage, another player on the team gets an adage, which he in turn must act out for his team to guess. The team that finishes its allotment of adages first wins.

Association

Players are seated in a circle around the room. One guest begins the game by mentioning a word. The next guest must say the first word that pops into his head. The third guest does the same, and so on around the room. The fun of the game is in seeing how far away from the first word the last one will be! For example, beginning with a simple word like "hot," you might get steam, pipe, smoke, cloud, sky-writing, airplane, flight, Atlantic, ocean, Europe.

Captions

Cut pictures out of newspapers or magazines and mount them on cardboard. Cut off the captions and paste them on the back. Show four guests the pictures. Supply them with pencils and paper, and have them write their own captions. The captions are then read aloud, along with the real captions on the backs. It will amuse your guests to see how different the captions will be!

Ad Scramble

Cut advertisements out of a magazine. Then cut off the copy from the illustration, leaving a picture with no message. Pictures and copy of 6 or more ads are then scrambled in the middle of a table. Guests try to match illustrations and "copy." It's fun and baffling. At the end of the time limit set, the guest with the most completed ads correctly matched is declared the winner.

Celebrity Race

Give each couple an envelope containing the picture of a well-known personality. The picture should be cut into ten pieces. The couple putting together the picture first, and identifying it, wins.

Who Is It?

The guest who is IT leaves the room while the others decide on the name of a famous person. When IT returns, he tries to identify the character by asking questions that may only be answered by YES or NO. All questions must be answered correctly. IT tries to guess the name of the character. He may ask such questions as, "Is it a man," "Does it live now," "Does it live in this country," "Is it famous in the field of sports." A time limit should be decided at the start of the game. When identification is made another guest takes his turn, and another famous name is chosen.

CHAPTER NINE

A WORD IN TIME!

A gracious and confident host is ready with the right word at the right moment. He puts his guests at ease — makes them feel welcome.

Here is a handy collection of winning toasts. You're certain to find many to please your guests.

FOREIGN TOASTS

"Here's to You"
in 15 Languages

American	—	Here's Luck!
British	—	Cheers!
Chinese	—	Wen Lie!
French	—	A votre sante!
German	—	Prosit!
Greek	—	Yasas!
Hebrew	—	L'Chayim!
Hungarian	—	Ege'sze'ge're!
Irish	—	Slainte!
Italian	—	Alla Salute!
Japanese	—	Kanpai!
Polish	—	Na Zdrowie!
Russian	—	Za vashe zdorovye!
Spanish	—	Salud!
Swedish	—	Skal!

CHAPTER TEN

WHISKEY WIT AND WISDOM

What is whiskey? Where does it come from?

Here are the facts — and a few fascinating tales which trace its colorful history.

What is Proof?

Proof is not an indication of quality. It is the measure of alcoholic content of a beverage. Early distillers had their own test. They mixed one-half gunpowder and one-half whiskey.

If the powder did not ignite when they applied a match to the mixture, it was too weak. If it did ignite and the flame burned too brightly it was too strong. But if it burned with a steady blue flame, it was said to be "proved." Usually that mixture was about 50% alcohol by volume.

Today proof of alcoholic content is measured much more exactly. Each degree of proof is one-half of one per cent of alcohol. An 86 proof whiskey, for example, contains 43% alcohol.

Taste in Whiskey

The distinctive taste in whiskey is achieved through the careful, painstaking art of blending. The knowledge of the blending expert is what gives good whiskies their consistent standard of smooth taste. Blending allows you to enjoy the same fine flavor again and again.

Whiskey In The American Tradition

It is reputed that the name cocktail originated in a tavern near New York around 1788. When American and French army officers came to the tavern known as "Betsy's Tavern," Betsy, the barmaid, would serve them a concoction of mixed spirits called "bracers."

Often the officers would tease the barmaid about the plump juicy chickens owned by a Tory neighbor. She threatened to make them eat their words.

One day they were served a chicken feast. When the officers had eaten their fill, and stepped to the bar, they found each glass of bracers decorated with a cock's tail from the Tory's rooster.

One Frenchman laughed, lifted his glass and said "Vive le cocktail." From then on, bracers were called cocktails.

Legends and Anecdotes About Whiskey

Whiskey may not be the oldest alcoholic beverage, but in America it is the most important one.

Whiskey historians tell us that it was the Irish, around 550 A.D., who were the first to be skilled in the arts of distillation.

Their product was called "uisgebeatha" or "usquebaugh" which were local translations from "water of life," aqua vitae in Latin. The English called it Whiskey. At that time, whiskey was used principally for medicinal purposes. It was first distilled on a broad scale by monks, surgeons or "Barboura" until early in the 16th Century when domestic distillation became common.

Today, Scotch, American and Canadian whiskies represent the main group of the world-famous beverage.

Scotch whisky is blended much in the same way as fine American spirit blends, like Calvert. But Scotch has a smoky flavor because the barley malt is exposed to smoke from a peat fire.

Irish Whiskey has a very strong flavor that is generally too strong for most palates.

Scotch and Irish whiskies are aged in used casks. They usually require longer aging than American whiskies.

Blended whiskies are known and respected for their consistent flavor and good taste. Blended whiskey, like Calvert, is the largest selling type of whiskey in the world. Most people prefer blended whiskey whether they drink it straight, in highballs or mixed drinks.

The Story of Calvert Extra, The Soft Whiskey

Calvert begins with the selection of premium grains. Corn, rye, and barley malt, rich in starch and potential flavor, are the basic materials in the production of whiskey and spirits. The proportions of corn to rye to barley malt will be varied to produce different flavor characteristics. By the same token, the time of cooking, the type of yeast, the distillation, and maturing—all influence the flavor of the individual whiskies and spirits which are blended together to produce Calvert Extra.

First, Calvert mills the corn and rye grains to expose more starch surface to the cooking process. Then water is added to the grain to make a *mash*, and the mash is cooked, slowly so that none of the grain is scorched. Next, *malt* is added, and the malt enzymes convert the starch to grain sugars. Malt is barley which has begun to germinate and form the remarkable enzyme substances which can convert starch into grain sugar.

After the converted mash is pumped to the fermenting tanks, one of Calvert's several hundred pedigreed *yeast* strains is added. Each strain of yeast can produce different flavor characteristics. As these millions of living cells multiply, the *fermentation* process begins, changing the grain sugars into ethyl alcohol, producing at the same time minute amounts of the flavor *congeners* which are the heart of the whiskey (along with the ethyl alcohol).

The fermented mash is *distilled* to separate the ethyl alcohol and flavor congeners from the grain husks and water. Distilling concentrates the flavors and raises the proof. In the production of whiskey, this process occurs at less than 160 proof.

When the same fermented mash is distilled at 190 proof or over, the result is a highly refined distillate called grain neutral *spirits*.

Whiskey is aged in new, charred white oak barrels, and with the interplay between whiskey and barrel, a very smooth and mellow product results at the proper moment of maturity.

Similarly, the unique spirits for Calvert Extra are stored in seasoned whiskey barrels for at least four years while they improve in the same general manner as straight whiskies. These distinctive Calvert spirits are made in a slow batch method called the "column and kettle" process, which leaves some delicate flavors in the spirits instead of stripping them bare of all flavor the way other spirits are made.

Only the center run of each batch of spirits goes into a barrel; but not a new barrel. That action would be too robust for the delicate spirit flavors. Calvert Extra spirits are stored in seasoned barrels which are selected from the thousands previously used for aging our straight whiskies.

Every few months, samples of each batch of straight whiskey and spirits are sent to Calvert's Library of Whiskies, where blenders maintain current samples of the thousands of distillates maturing in Calvert warehouses to make certain that each whiskey or spirit is taken at its peak of flavor.

After four or five years, not just one variety of spirits, but many, made in different Calvert distilleries which produce different flavor characteristics, are blended with a variety of Calvert straight whiskies of various ages to produce a blend which combines the best characteristics of each ingredient—Calvert Extra.

Only by starting with our exclusive improved spirits can we achieve the extra dimension of lightness combined with depth which distinguishes Calvert Extra. Only the artistry and skill borne of generations of experience here and abroad, drawing on the tremendous inventory resources of the Calvert company, could produce Calvert Extra, the Soft Whiskey.

The Story of Canadian Lord Calvert

Canadian Lord Calvert is a blend of fine aged whiskies produced under Canadian government supervision in our five distilleries in Canada. By bringing it across the border in barrels, we save on taxes and freight and pass the savings on to you in a price that is lower than that of any other Canadian whisky of comparable quality.

Each of our five Canadian distilleries yields whiskies with distinctive flavor characteristics which contribute to the final taste. Even the same basic "recipe" would produce a different flavor at each of the five plants, because of differences in climate, equipment, warehouses, and water. For example, at New Westminster whiskies are made with the soft, almost sweet, water from the slopes of the Rockies, while at Beaupre the whiskies are made with limestone spring water from the Laurentian Mountains.

Only Canadian Lord Calvert includes bright whiskies from New Westminster in British Columbia, full-bodied whiskies from Ville la Salle in Quebec, rich whiskies from Waterloo and Amherstburg in Ontario, and golden whiskies from Quebec's Beaupre in a unique blend of subtle lightness.

The individual whiskies for Lord Calvert are produced in four different types of stills: *continuous stills* for the lightest, most delicate whiskies, *column and kettle batch stills* for somewhat more flavorful whiskies which are the heart of Canadian Lord Calvert, and *primary whisky stills* for more robust bourbon and rye flavors. At our Montreal plant, North America's only *"Coffey" still,* a type developed a hundred years ago by the Scotsman Aeneas Coffey, produces unique whisky flavors which add the finishing touch to Canadian Lord Calvert.

Our skilled blenders draw on this huge variety of whisky flavors from all across Canada to create the extraordinary taste of Canadian Lord Calvert. Only Calvert, with five strategically located distilleries in Canada, can bring you the remarkable flavor of Canadian Lord Calvert.

The Calvert Gin Story

Today's discerning drinker demands a completely dry gin without a trace of sweetness or "perfume." Calvert 100% Dry Gin was created especially to satisfy this careful buyer who is determined to have the finest.

Gin has been made for more than three hundred years, but about the only link between the gin of today and centuries ago is the juniper berry which gives gin its characteristic aroma.

Today's Calvert gin contains hints of nearly a dozen botanicals, all combined on a base of the purest grain neutral spirits. Coriander, cassia, angelica, anise . . . all contribute tiny whispers of taste and aroma to the finished gin. But then Calvert adds an exclusive "secret ingredient" used by no other distiller: fresh lime peel. The lime peel produces a fresh crispness in Calvert Gin which no other gin enjoys.

Although skill and experience in choosing and marrying botanicals are obviously important to the final flavor of the gin, even before he begins to work with botanicals, the distiller must have a 100% dry spirit or his gin can never be dry enough to suit the discerning drinker.

Calvert spirits are distilled through six modern still columns. At each distillation perfume-y "heads" and "tails" flavors are drawn off and discarded. Only the center run "dry zone" spirits are kept, becoming dryer at each new distillation.

Finally, these 100% dry spirits are distilled a seventh time, this time in a "gin head" still with carefully measured and balanced botanicals. Once again only the dry center run of the distillation is saved for bottling as Calvert 100% Dry Gin.

Why Calvert Cocktails are "Goof-proof"

Up to now to get perfect mixed drinks you had to be buddies with the bartender. But not any longer—not with Calvert ready-to-serve Cocktails! It took four years to make them goof-proof.

Our secret is: Make everything that goes into the cocktails yourself. And make it good. Take our Whiskey Sour. Made with Calvert Extra, the Soft Whiskey, plus lemon and orange. Sound easy? It isn't. If you put fresh juice into a bottled cocktail, in no time you'll have a broken down drink with a funny color and a funny taste.

What we do is buy our own fruit. Then actually distill a fresh fruit essence in our unique "cocktail still." The result is a Whiskey Sour that tastes as if your bartender friend just poured it.

To get a great Daiquiri, we had to make a great rum. It's the first rum ever made in the Hawaiian Islands and it makes a humdinger of a Daiquiri.

The Martini? Calvert 100% dry gin and our own extra extra dry vermouth. It took years to make that vermouth. A lot of work, but worth it. There isn't a mean streak in our Martini. It purrs when you pour it over ice.

Our Manhattan, of course, is a Soft Manhattan, made with Calvert Extra. And just a splash of our not-too-sweet vermouth. Even after the bottle is opened, every Calvert Cocktail keeps its freshness because the ingredients are distilled by a special process. And that's it. You couldn't goof 'em if you tried.

INDEX OF DRINKS

INDEX OF DRINKS

95

INDEX OF DRINKS